Alberto Bertolazzi

Illustrations by Erika De Pieri

SOCCER FOR KiDS

An Illustrated Guide

Meyer & Meyer Sport

CONTENTS

HISTORY AND GEOGRAPHY OF SOCCER

A LITTLE HISTORY

Soccer is the most practiced, widespread, and followed sport in the world. According to the most recent statistics, more than a billion people play it, it has more than 5 billion potential spectators, and it is played in almost every country on earth. It is enjoyed by children and adults, men and women, outdoors or indoors. And people have been playing it for over 2,000 years!

➤ The sport most similar to what we know as soccer, from the third century BC, was Chinese *cuju*, in which players had to kick a ball filled with feathers and hair between two bamboo canes.

➤ About 500 years later, *kemari* was played in Japan: players had to prevent the ball from touching the ground using only their feet.

➤ The Greeks played *episkyros* – which the Romans called *harpastum* – in which the object was to get a ball over the opposition's last line.

➤ With more or less the same rules, in the Middle Ages people played Florentine soccer, which is still practiced today.

➤ Modern soccer was invented in English boarding schools around the middle of the nineteenth century.

WHERE IS IT PLAYED?

Soccer is played practically everywhere, from the Himalayan valleys to the African deserts. But there are countries where the number of players is enormous. Which ones? The USA, China, Brazil, Russia... Then there are the traditionally leading nations in this sport, home to the most important championships and most famous teams: Brazil, Argentina, Uruguay, England, France, Italy, Spain, Germany...

WHO PLAYS IT?

Men and women, children and adults, the able-bodied and the disabled: soccer is played by everyone at all ages, so there is an infinity of games and events. Adult men's soccer is the one that attracts the greatest sporting and economic interest, but in recent years there has been increased attention paid to youth competitions and women's soccer, which is very popular in English-speaking countries and Northern and Central Europe.

11, 7, 5-A-SIDE...

Soccer, in its most popular version, involves teams of 11 players and outdoor grass fields, or pitches. But in every country the climate and local traditions have produced variations.

A very popular variant is futsal, which is played indoors, 5 against 5 (known as "5-a-side"). In warmer countries, beach soccer is popular, played in teams of 5 on the sand and strictly barefoot...

WHO DECIDES THE RULES OF THE GAME?

As in other sports, competitive-level soccer has a number of controlling bodies. The most important are: FIFA, based in Switzerland, which runs world soccer and organizes the World Cup; UEFA, which manages European soccer and organizes the Champions League; IFAB which administers and establishes the rules of soccer.

THE FANS

Among soccer lovers, there are many who, as well as practicing the sport, love to watch it at the stadium or on TV. Many of them support a particular team and are called "fans;" they wear their favorite player's top, sing the team songs and wave flags with their beloved colors... When they go too far and live only to support their own team, they are called "ultras." If they are also violent and, stupidly, instead of watching the game prefer to fight with other fans, they are called "hooligans."

GETTING STARTED

TEN THINGS TO KNOW

▶ The aim of the game is to score GOOOALS

▶ Whoever scores more goals wins

▶ It is played 11 vs. 11

▶ To score it is necessary to put the ball into the goal

▶ Players cannot use their hands (except the goalkeeper)

▶ Usually feet are used, but also head, chest, and knees

▶ It is played outdoors on a grass pitch (natural or synthetic)

▶ There is a referee who applies the rules

▶ There is one ball and everyone wants it...

▶ The match lasts 90 minutes (split into two halves)

1ST HALF 45'

2ND HALF 45'

HALF-TIME: 15'

INJURY TIME: A FEW MINUTES

THE BASIC EQUIPMENT

SOCCER BALL

The ball is the only really indispensable item in soccer! It is a sphere ranging from 27 to 28 inches in circumference, made of leather or synthetic material; its weight can vary from 14 to 16 ounces.

SOCCER CLEATS

Once they were made of hide or leather, now they are made with synthetic, soft, and durable materials. Beneath the sole are the studs, made of different materials and in varying numbers depending on their purpose: from 8 to 13 if they are fixed and plastic, to be used on hard ground; from 6 to 8 if they are metal, used on soft ground. The length of the studs must not exceed 3/4 inches.

GOALKEEPER'S GLOVES

Goalkeepers usually wear gloves, which serve both to protect their hands from the more powerful shots and to help stop the ball.

SHIN GUARDS

Shin guards are used to protect the lower leg from kicks... They are made with various types of materials, including foam, polyurethane, and other types of plastic.

CAPTAIN'S ARMBAND

Each team has a captain who is authorized to speak with the referee. They can be identified by their armband.

THE PITCH

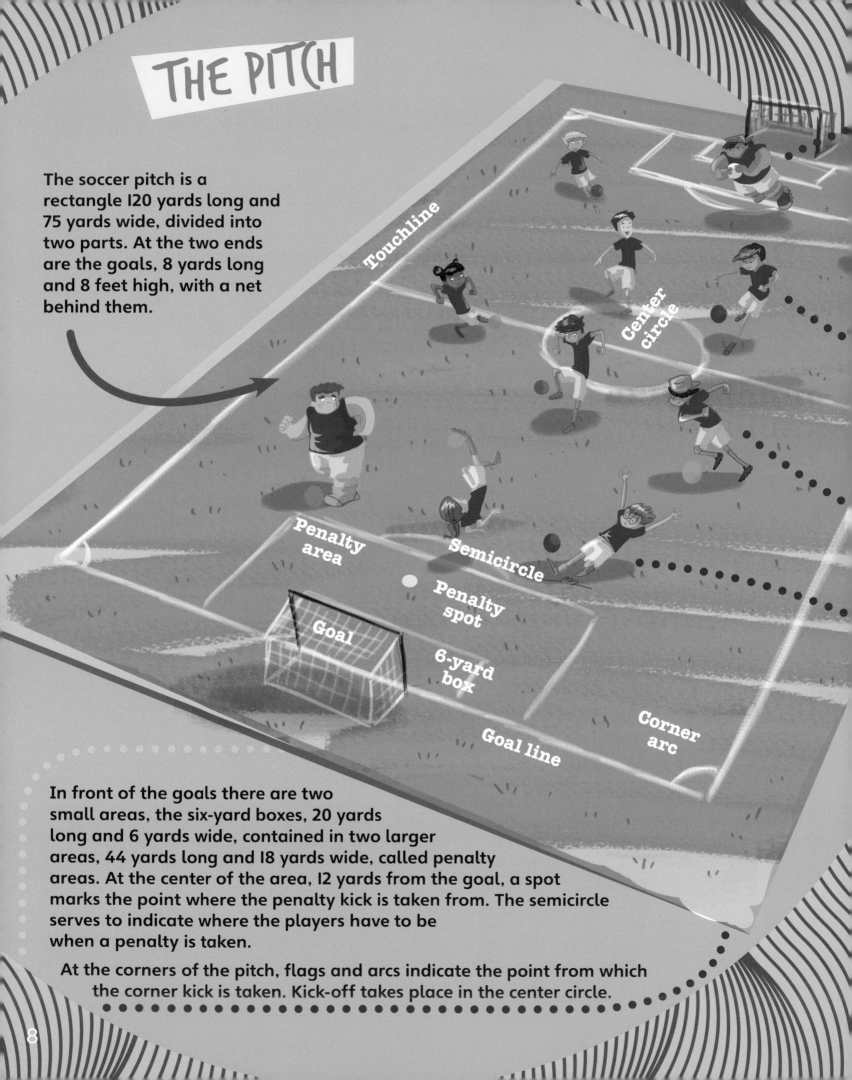

The soccer pitch is a rectangle 120 yards long and 75 yards wide, divided into two parts. At the two ends are the goals, 8 yards long and 8 feet high, with a net behind them.

Touchline

Center circle

Penalty area

Semicircle

Penalty spot

Goal

6-yard box

Goal line

Corner arc

In front of the goals there are two small areas, the six-yard boxes, 20 yards long and 6 yards wide, contained in two larger areas, 44 yards long and 18 yards wide, called penalty areas. At the center of the area, 12 yards from the goal, a spot marks the point where the penalty kick is taken from. The semicircle serves to indicate where the players have to be when a penalty is taken.

At the corners of the pitch, flags and arcs indicate the point from which the corner kick is taken. Kick-off takes place in the center circle.

THE ROLES

GOALKEEPER

The only player who can touch the ball with their hands in the penalty area. Their job is to keep the ball from entering the goal.

DEFENDERS

Above all, they have to prevent the players of the other team from shooting and scoring, but in modern soccer they also help midfielders and strikers try to score. They are divided into central defenders (once called stoppers and sweepers) and side backs (once called full backs).

MIDFIELDERS

They are the all-rounders of soccer: they have to defend and attack, run a lot, and build the game up, that is, take the ball, carry it forward, and pass it to the attackers. So they have to be part artist and part warrior. They are divided into central and outside midfielders; once they were called the playmaker (the player who set the tempo of the game), the halfback (who defended and ran the most), and the inside forward (who attacked most).

ATTACKERS

Their aim is to score! But in modern soccer they have to help the team when it defends as well. They are divided into central attackers (sometimes called the center-forward whose role above all is to score) and wingers who dribble and cross, but often try to score goals themselves.

THE REFEREES

In professional soccer just one referee is not enough: they need 6!

THE MAIN REFEREE

They make the decisions, run on the pitch, and try to be as close as possible to where the ball is. In professional soccer they are connected to the other referees with a microphone and an earpiece.

THE ASSISTANT REFEREES

There are two of them and they follow play from the sidelines. They have a flag with which they signal significant fouls and offside positions.

ADDITIONAL ASSISTANT REFEREES

There are two of them and they follow the game from the side of the pitch, near the goals. They signal penalty fouls by microphone and help the main referee decide if the ball has crossed the line or not.

VIDEO ASSISTANT REFEREE

They spend the whole game in front of a monitor checking and rechecking TV footage of the match. They intervene when the main referee asks them to or if important situations arise that the main referee has not seen.

THE CARDS

The main referee has a whistle with which they stop the game in the event of a foul, a goal, or the end of a half. They also have two cards, one yellow and one red, with which they signal warnings or expulsions. On the back of the cards there is space to write the names or numbers of the players who are warned or sent off.

YELLOW CARD

The referee shows a yellow card to a player to warn them: this happens when the player commits fairly serious, or repeated, fouls. Two yellow cards equal a red card.

RED CARD

The referee shows the red card to a player to expel them, that is, to send them off the pitch for the rest of the game: this happens when the player commits very serious, dangerous, or unsporting fouls.

THE MAIN RULES

WHAT NOT TO DO

When you play soccer, there are some things you absolutely cannot do:

➤ Touch the ball with your hands or your arms (unless you are the goalkeeper, or if you are taking a throw-in when the ball has gone out of play on the sideline);

➤ trip opponents;

➤ kick opponents (or attempt to);

➤ strike opponents with fists or elbows (or attempt to);

➤ violently charge opponents from behind;

➤ hold opponents with the hands and arms;

➤ in general, play in a dangerous way (including tackling in a way that is too violent);

➤ kick the ball away after the referee has stopped the game;

➤ insult or attack opponents or the referee;

➤ have 12 players on the field (the referee can suspend the match);

➤ enter or leave the field without the referee's permission;

➤ pretend to have been fouled (lots of players do this, but if the referee realizes they will give a foul against you and give you a yellow card).

OFFSIDE

In soccer there is a special rule: offside. Here is how it works:

➤ a player is in an offside position if, at the time the pass is made, there are not at least two players from the other team between them and the opposing goal line.

But it is not offside when:

➤ the player receives the ball in their own half of the pitch;

➤ the ball was last touched by an opponent;

➤ the ball comes directly from a corner kick or a throw-in;

➤ the ball was put back into play by the referee.

FOULS

WHEN YOU COMMIT A FOUL, THE REFEREE WHISTLES FOR A PENALTY AGAINST YOU. BUT WHAT PENALTY?

➤ If you commit a foul in your own penalty area, the referee whistles for a penalty kick against your team: one of your opponents can place the ball on the penalty spot and shoot at goal without anyone in their way.

➤ If you commit the same foul in any other part of the pitch, the referee can whistle for a direct free kick (your opponent can kick at goal) or indirect (at least two touches of the ball before shooting), but you can form a wall with your teammates.

IN PLAY, NOT IN PLAY

When the ball is not in play it is impossible to score. But... how do we know when it is not in play?

➤ When the referee has whistled for a foul (it will be put back into play with a free kick).

➤ When the referee has whistled for a suspension of the game (the ball will be put back into the game directly by the referee with a drop ball).

➤ When the ball goes out of the pitch (it will be put back into play with the hands if it crossed a sideline, with the feet if it crossed the goal line).

➤ When one of the teams has scored (it will be put back into play in the center circle).

➤ When the referee has whistled for the end of the half.

CURIOSITIES

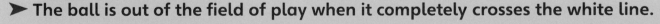

➤ The ball is out of the field of play when it completely crosses the white line.

➤ Players cannot wear rings, chains, or other dangerous items.

➤ Teams must always be recognizable, so the referee can have a team change jerseys if there is a risk of confusion.

➤ If the ball does not bounce because the pitch is unplayable, the referee may suspend or postpone the match.

➤ If anyone other than the players enters the pitch, the referee may suspend the match.

➤ At free kicks, the ball is in play once it rolls 360 degrees.

INDIVIDUAL TECHNIQUES

OUTFIELD PLAYERS

KICKING THE BALL

Hitting the soccer ball with the feet is one of the basic techniques of soccer. It serves to pass the ball to a teammate and also to shoot at goal to score. But there is not just one way to kick. Usually, players employ these four techniques:

SIDE FOOT

The side of the foot is the part that goes from the heel to the big toe on the inside of the foot.
It is the largest surface we have available to hit the ball, so it is also the ideal instrument to kick with precision. This technique has one defect: it is difficult to get a lot of power with a side kick and it is usually shorter than a kick using the instep.

THE SECRET: rotate the leg and the ankle outward so that the side of the foot is pointing exactly at the target; the ankle must be rigid at the moment of impact; the further back you pull your leg, the further the ball will travel.

INSIDE FOOT

The inside of the foot is the surface that goes from the middle of the foot to the big toe. It is a surface that allows a kick that is both precise and powerful. The inside foot is used especially to give the ball a inward direction (i.e., curving to the left if kicking with the right or to the right if kicking with the left).

THE SECRET: keep the ankle rigid and stretch the tip of the foot under the ball; hold the supporting leg slightly bent in order to ensure maximum balance; hit the external part of the ball.

OUTSIDE FOOT

The outside foot is the part that goes from the ankle to the little toe and consists of the outside of the instep. It is a fairly rigid but not too large a surface, so the pass made with the outside is not always accurate. The outside foot is mainly used to give the ball an outward direction (i.e., curving to the left if kicking with the left or to the right if kicking with the right).

THE SECRET: stretch the instep inwards, so as to offer the largest possible external surface; hit the internal part of the ball; after impact, slide the leg inwards.

INSTEP

The instep of the foot is an extended and rigid surface that goes from the ankle to the toes: kicking with the instep allows players to make a long pass, but requires a lot of training for it to be accurate as well. Kicked with the instep, the ball usually moves in a straight line but, with the proper technique, it is possible to give it a reverse spin; in this way the trajectory rises and stretches, and the ball stops at the point where it bounces, facilitating the stop for the player receiving it.

THE SECRET: keep the supporting leg bent; hold the ankle rigid and the tip of the foot extended forward; hit the ball in the center for power, and in the lower part to give it reverse spin.

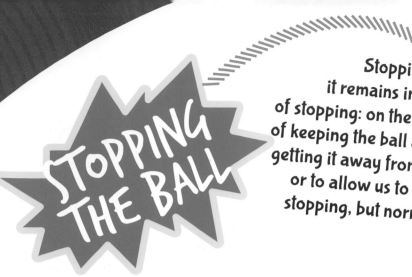

STOPPING THE BALL

Stopping the ball means controlling it so that it remains in our possession. There are two main ways of stopping: on the spot and following through. The first has the aim of keeping the ball as close as possible to our feet, the second that of getting it away from us in a controlled way, to get past an opponent or to allow us to shoot at goal. Any part of the body is fine for stopping, but normally the ball is controlled in these four ways:

WITH THE SIDE OF THE FOOT

The side of the foot is the widest and most sensitive surface at our disposal. Stopping with the side of the foot allows precise control. This technique is always used when the ball is arriving fast and at ground level. Simply rotate the leg and point the ankle outwards to provide the maximum surface of the side of the foot to the ball.

THE SECRET: keep the ankle relaxed and slightly lower the foot when the ball arrives; lean on the supporting leg in order to ensure maximum balance; in general, make sure to cover the ball with the body.

WITH THE INSTEP

Stopping with the instep requires a lot of sensitivity and a relaxed ankle. Use the instep when the ball comes from a height or when we want to keep it in the air. It is not easy to achieve accurate control because the instep is a rigid surface and the ball tends to bounce a distance away, but with exercise this stop enables us to play in a more elegant and technical way.

THE SECRET: raise the foot towards the falling ball, keeping the ankle relaxed, and follow the trajectory, letting it slowly run down the foot on impact; better players also use the supporting leg, folding it to cushion the ball.

WITH THE THIGH

If the ball arrives high and suddenly, there is often no time to stop it using the feet. If the ball is a chip (i.e., dropping down), it is possible to use the thigh: simply raise the knee and ensure the thigh offers a large and soft horizontal surface on which the ball will just bounce before immediately dropping to the ground near the feet.

THE SECRET:

open the arms and bend the supporting leg for better balance; cushion the rebound by slightly lowering the thigh at the precise moment of impact with the ball.

WITH THE CHEST

When the ball arrives high, but is not quite a chip, there is no time to stop it either with the feet or the thigh. Then it is possible to take up a position in order to let it bounce on the upper chest just above the sternum.

Simply open the arms, turn the chest in the direction of the ball and lean slightly with the head back in order to offer the maximum surface to the ball.

THE SECRET:

tilt your chest upwards and breathe in if the idea is to kick the ball away after the stop; tilt your chest down and deflate if you want to place the ball on the ground; use the legs as well, folding them to cushion the ball.

PASSING

Passing is the way in which team play is developed; every time a player is placed under pressure by an opponent or a teammate is in a better position than our own, we pass the ball.

Of course it is possible to pass the ball with every part of the body, but here we focus on techniques using the feet.

THE ONE-TOUCH PASS

A one-touch pass means hitting the ball without stopping it; this is done to speed up play and surprise the opponent. Since it is fairly difficult, the ball is usually struck with the side of the foot; this is more accurate, but the pass will be shorter.

THE SECRET: hit the ball with as much of the side of the foot as possible; allow the ball to come as close to the supporting leg as possible.

THE LONG PASS

The long pass delivers the ball to a teammate at a distance but in a favorable position. The idea is to hit the ball with the instep; to increase the trajectory it is possible to apply a reverse spin, that is, an effect which also makes the bounce on the ground easier to control.

THE SECRET: to give the ball a reverse spin, it needs to be struck in the lower part, stretching the top of the foot under the ball; to increase power, the kicking leg has to be pulled back.

THE ASSIST

The "assist" is the pass that delivers the ball to a teammate who is able to score. Often it is a short pass, but one that is difficult to pull off because it is done in the heart of the opposition defense: a chip, along the ground, a back-heeler...

THE SECRET: to give the pass the greatest accuracy, strike the ball with the instep or inside of the foot.

The shot comes at the end of a move and is perhaps one of the most exciting moments of the game because shots can turn into goals! Shooting requires precision, power, and sense of timing; if one of these components is missing, a good goalkeeper will not have any difficulty saving your shots...

Of course it is also possible to shoot at the goal with the heel, knee, or chest, but we will focus on techniques using the feet:

ON THE HALF-VOLLEY

Striking the ball on the half-volley means kicking it right after it bounces on the ground when the ball is still rising. By doing so, players take advantage of the kinetic energy to give more power to the shot and steal time from the goalkeeper, but it is harder to be precise.

THE SECRET:
cover the ball with the body so that it is very close to the supporting foot, and strike it with the instep.

THE OVERHEAD KICK

The overhead kick, like any acrobatic stunt, is a highly spectacular shot that allows us to hit the ball when it is high in front of us, but the goal is behind us. To give strength to the kick it is necessary to use the instep.

THE SECRET:
leap and then first fling the supporting leg; only later pull back the leg that is being used to kick; hold an arm pointing to the ground to cushion the fall.

ON THE VOLLEY

When the ball comes towards us and there is no time to stop it, we are forced to hit it on the volley. If the ball is at ground level we can use the side of the foot, which is more accurate, but if the ball is in flight, or if we want to give it a lot of power, we have to strike it with the instep.

THE SECRET:
use the arms to keep the balance; wait for the ball to come close to the body: the farther away it is struck, the less accurate the kick will be.

HEADER

The header allows us to hit the ball when it is still very high, cannot be reached with the feet, or stopped with any part of the body. With the header players can defend, pass the ball to a teammate, or aim for goal to score.

Generally, the best headers of the ball are tall.

But since the header also requires power and timing,

some shorter players can also be very good at this skill.

WHEN TO USE THE HEAD

In defense we use the header to move the ball away from our goal. This happens when we are in the penalty area and the ball comes from the side (a cross or corner kick), or when an opponent passes the ball long and high to a striker and we intercept the pass. In attack, we use the header to pass the ball to a teammate or to fire it directly at the goal, from a cross from a teammate.

THE SECRET: calculate the trajectory of the ball well and try to anticipate the opponent; open the arms to maintain balance and keep opponents away; we look at the position of our teammates or the opposing goalkeeper while the ball is still in flight.

HOW TO JUMP

To anticipate the opponent and avoid the ball passing over us, we often have to jump. Depending on the time and space we have, we jump on two feet or use the running header. In the first case, we have to use our legs as though they were springs, bending them for power and throwing the arms upwards when we jump; in the second case we have to take a short run and push with one leg, again using the arms to give us momentum for jumping. The second technique normally allows us to jump higher and more dynamically, so it is ideal, especially if we are attacking.

THE SECRET: use the arms well to get more momentum and balance and keep opponents away; arch the back for a more powerful impact with the ball.

HOW TO HIT THE BALL

The ball can be hit with any part of the head. As can be easily guessed, the forehead, offering a wider surface, is more precise. Also, when we meet the ball frontally, we can follow its trajectory until we strike it. Sometimes, however, the ball arrives very quickly and we cannot take up the best position; in that case, to pass to a teammate or surprise the goalkeeper, we can touch it with the nape of the neck or the side of the forehead.

THE SECRET: use the hands to aim at the ball and force us to keep our forehead facing the ball; strike with the center of the forehead for greater power and precision; strengthen the header by bringing the head back and opening the chest; tighten the neck muscles on impact.

Hitting the ball with the center of the forehead makes impact painless and the shot more precise and powerful.

Extend the arms and legs for better balance and to keep opponents away.

Two feet

Running header

DRIBBLING

Dribbling is a movement with the ball that allows us to pass an opponent preventing us from passing or aiming for goal.

How to dribble past an opponent? There is not just one way; it is possible to move the ball away and then retrieve it (with a chip or by knocking the ball forward and passing the opponent at speed), or keeping it glued to the foot, using dummies, and any other moves we can think of.

WHEN TO USE DRIBBLING

Leaving an opponent behind is fun and looks good, but sometimes the game is not worth the risk; teachers and coaches therefore generally ask that dribbling be used only when it is necessary. So when is that? When an opponent is putting pressure on us and leaves us no room to advance, pass the ball, or shoot; when it is the only way to create a threat; when successful dribbling allows us to get into in a favorable position to score; when any mistake in dribbling does not cause an immediate threat to our own goal.
(Never dribble in your own penalty area!)

THE SECRET: dribble only if it is the best option available; try it only if it is one-against-one; before doing so, evaluate carefully the position of teammates and opponents.

CONTROL

If we are not sure of being faster than the opponent, we have to keep the ball near us. Keeping the ball as close to the feet as possible while running fast requires a lot of practice and a fair share of sensitivity; the ankle has to be relaxed and the knees bent so as to lower the center of gravity of the body and allow better coverage of the ball. The touch can be with either the inside or outside of the foot; the ideal is to alternate outside and inside, thus moving the ball from a two-footed internal position (safer but predictable) to an external position (less safe but more unpredictable).

THE DUMMY

Holding the ball close to the feet we offer an easier target to the defender, so we have to invent something to be able to get past them. The best dribblers use the so-called dummy, that is, they seek to deceive the opponent by making them believe something that they then do not do. They move the ball to the left, for example, then race to the right; or pretend to pass it and then run off quickly. The dummy works best when using the whole body; for this reason it is necessary to have full control of the ball, legs, hips, and trunk.

THE SECRET: being able to control the ball with two feet, both the inside and outside, increases the number of choices to dribble past opponents; running at speed, it is better to control with the outside because the surface is softer and the ankle makes a more natural movement.

THE SECRET: keeping the knees very bent and the trunk leaning forwards improves balance and allows the use of the most common dummy, that is, the right-left shift.

THE CHANGE OF PACE

Controlling the ball well and knowing how to dummy may not be enough to get past a good defender. In this case, it is also necessary to know how to change pace: alternating, for example, our speed; moving quickly from a standing start and then stopping immediately; or changing the frequency of the run or the amplitude of the step. The change of tempo increases the variables that our opponent has to control and therefore makes our dummies more unpredictable.

THE SECRET: the ability to change pace depends more on elasticity than power, so it is advisable to exercise the ankles which transform the energy of the leg muscles into elastic force.

DEFENDING THE BALL

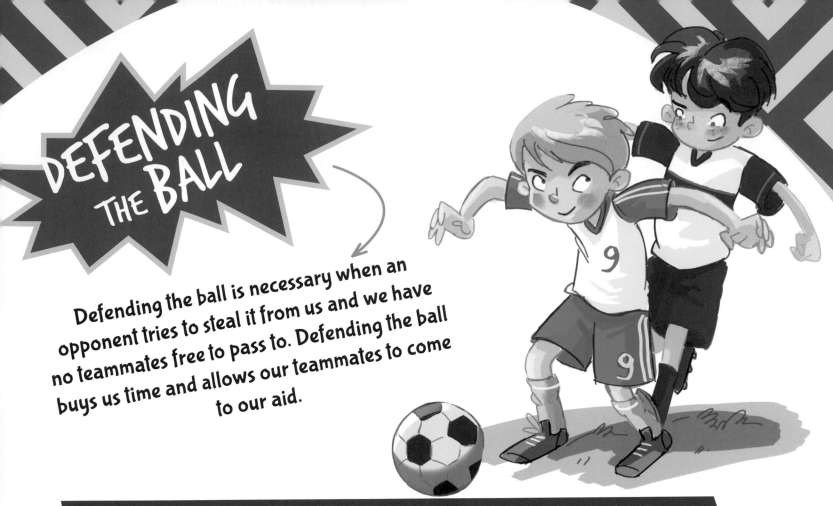

Defending the ball is necessary when an opponent tries to steal it from us and we have no teammates free to pass to. Defending the ball buys us time and allows our teammates to come to our aid.

There are two main techniques for defending the ball: putting our body between the opponent and the ball, or moving the ball so that the opponent cannot touch it.

USING THE BODY AS A BARRIER

Under the rules the body can be used to protect the ball. Shielding when the defender approaches forces them to look for space to reach the ball, an attempt that often turns into a foul in our favor. The use of legs, shoulders, and arms is permitted to keep an opponent away from the ball, as long as they are not pushed or hit. The most common technique is for players to turn their back on the opponent and cover the ball, keeping it between their legs, at a safe distance. Usually they try to keep the ball on the foot further away from the opponent.

THE SECRET: use open arms only to increase the surface of the barrier, not to push or move the opponent; keep the legs bent and stable, to withstand the opponent's pressure; move the ball away from the feet as much as is required for it not to be in reach of the opponent and to force them to come around us.

WATCHING OUT OF THE CORNER OF THE EYE

Beginners, above all, tend to focus their attention on the ball when defending it; this can be a mistake, because they lose sight of the movements of our teammates and opponents. To be fully aware of what is happening on the field and to see in advance the moves of those who are trying to steal the ball from us and the teammates who are free to receive a pass, it is a good idea to get used to watching the ball only out of the corner of the eye or at least keeping it in our peripheral vision.

THE SECRET:

keep the ball glued to the outside of the foot so as to be able see it out of the corner of the eye without losing sight of the field of play.

MOVING THE BALL

When an opponent attacks us, we can prevent them from stealing the ball by continually moving it, so that it is never in range of being taken; this is a kind of defensive dribbling, not to provide us with space for maneuvering or shooting, but simply to keep possession of the ball. It can be done conservatively, moving the ball to bring it under our protective shield and using the body as a barrier (see facing page); or it can become offensive dribbling, which happens when we take advantage of the opponent's imbalance to get past them and race off, ball at the feet, in attack.

THE SECRET:

usually the inside of the foot is used to move the ball beneath our protective shield; instead the outside of the foot is used to pass the opponent and exploit their lack of balance to begin an attack.

WINNING THE BALL

If the opponents are in possession of the ball, our aim is, firstly, to keep them from becoming a threat and, secondly, to recover possession of the ball. How to do this?

First of all, it should be remembered that defense is not just for defenders, but all the players in movement. If all the players try together to recover a ball, the objective will be easier to achieve. Of course it is also necessary to know how to use some individual techniques that will allow us to recover the ball without committing a foul.

THE TIME FACTOR

If we do not have teammates available to help us, it is a good idea to slow down the opponent in possession of the ball without attempting a tackle or slide. In fact, the time factor can be our ally, delaying the action of our opponents so we can organize ourselves, give our teammates time to return to the right position, or break up the tempo of the attack. In general, it is not always necessary to try to take the ball away from the opponent: sometimes it is enough to stand in front of them and wait for them to make a mistake, and then take advantage of it.

PLAYING AS A TEAM

When an attacker aims at a defender, they are likely to get past them if facing them individually. But if the defender plays as a member of team, they know where their teammates are and what is the best course of action: to retreat when they are alone; to attack if there is a teammate who can remedy their mistakes; to move in such a way as to impact the opponent's choices; to not try to mark all the attackers alone and be clear in asking for help; and to help a teammate in difficulty.

THE SECRET: to slow down the opponent, it is necessary to run beside them, remaining close enough to be able to take advantage of any errors in control or passing.

THE SECRET: look around and remember the position of opponents and teammates; imagine lines of possible passes and reduce the attacker's range of choice.

THE TACKLE

The tackle is the moment when we come into contact with the opponent and try to take control of the ball from them. The best way to tackle is to run parallel to the player holding the ball and not to wait for them frontally. The qualities to use for a good tackle are decisiveness (when tackling it is necessary to not pull the leg back) and timing (it is necessary to choose the right moment to intervene; this is usually immediately after a touch of ball from the player in possession, which creates a space to insert the foot).

Sometimes we might not think it, but it can be important to dummy the action because doing so will cause the opponent to dribble faster and so run a higher risk of making a mistake.

THE SECRET: stay low, with knees bent, ready to move with as much agility as possible; do not keep the legs too open, otherwise a capable opponent might take advantage of this to pass the ball between them (a tunnel); keep the eyes on the ball and not on the feet of the attacker.

THE SLIDING TACKLE

Sliding tackles are lovely to see and in many cases effective, but they are the riskiest choice available to a defender. A defender should go to the ground only when they have no way of defending on their feet: if the attacker is faster or very good at dribbling, for example, or if he does not have a the support of a teammate. In these cases, the sliding tackle, even if it does not provide the certainty of retrieving the ball, may give the rest of the team the chance to recover.

THE SECRET: never slow down before going to the ground, but rather accelerate before sliding, to give the sliding leg the right movement.

INDIVIDUAL TECHNIQUES

SPECIAL RULES

The goalkeeper is the only player allowed to touch the ball in play with his hands. Therefore, the goalkeeper has some special rules that need to be learned.

► The goalkeeper outside his own penalty area is a player like any other: they cannot use their hands.

► In the case of a voluntary pass back by a teammate (unless using head or chest), the goalkeeper cannot pick the ball up and has to play with their feet.

► The goalkeeper cannot hold the ball for more than 6 seconds.

► Having released the ball, the goalkeeper cannot touch it again with their hands until it has been touched by another player.

POSITIONING

A good goalkeeper is very attentive to positioning: the first objective is to close down the goalmouth, to give the shooter the least possible chance. Therefore, it is necessary to adjust to situations during the game: if the attacker is coming from the right, for example, it is necessary to leave the center of the goal and approach the right post, turning to the ball (but always checking what is happening on the rest of the pitch). Many goalkeepers move from the goal line and advance a few steps towards the ball, thus closing the goalmouth better, but risking being beaten by a chip. The goalkeeper also has to a evaluate their position in dead-ball situations: for corner kicks they need to place themselves in the center of the six-yard box and gain the space to jump and block the ball or knock it out; for free kicks they have to know how to position the wall so as to cover the goal; for penalty kicks they have to stand on the goal line but can move to fool the penalty taker with a dummy.

THE SAVE

The save is the goalkeeper's most important and spectacular act.

THE DIVING SAVE

Diving to the ground is one of the first things a goalkeeper has to learn to do. To do this well and to avoid unnecessary bruising, goalkeepers should start from a lowered position with their legs bent. If the ball is going to the right, it is necessary to take half a step in that direction, using the right leg for momentum and the left for push, and vice versa if the ball is going to the left. In the fall, the inside arm is bent to cushion the blow, unless the ball is so far away as to oblige us to keep the arm extended. If possible, we use the whole body to protect the goal, immediately closing our arms to block the ball after impact.

THE FLYING SAVE

When the ball is heading to the top corner of the goal, the only way to avoid the goal is... a flying save. This is a spectacular move, which requires a lot of physical training. The steps of the technique are: take half a step in the direction of the ball; use the outer leg for the push and the inner for thrust and momentum; stretch the arms to the maximum, with the hands open; falling down, fold the arms and use them to cushion the impact with the ground.

THE SECRET:

in order to not get hurt, many goalkeepers slide on their side after the impact with the ground, not unlike what volleyball players do. Obviously this works best if playing on grass...

THE SECRET:

it is not possible to slide to reduce the effects of falling after a flying save, so it is necessary to use arms and hands; the best goalkeepers can grab the ball and land using it as a cushion...

COMING OUT LOW

The goalkeeper coming out low is the equivalent of the defender's tackle; there are risks because usually it will involve throwing their arms and head between the attacker's feet.

TIMING

Timing is crucial! As defenders do, so too must goalkeepers wait for the attacker to touch the ball and move it away from their feet. At that point, they throw themselves quickly with their hands towards the ball, making sure to place their body across the way and not leave their legs behind them; this way they can use the whole body as a barrier and make it harder for the attacker to score or dribble.

BRAVERY

Leaping at the legs of an attacker requires courage. But courage is not madness! Coming out low must be practiced a lot in training, so as to be sure of the movements to carry out. In any case, not everyone can dive on the ball without any fear, so it is natural to be worried at first. This is the point of training: repeating the technical move over and over gives us confidence and removes the fear.

THE SECRET:
so as not to hurt the head, go with the arms and hands towards the ball, using them for protection as well.

THE SECRET:
at the beginning, go out with the legs forward, as if for a sliding tackle; gradually it will become natural to bring the arms and hands forward.

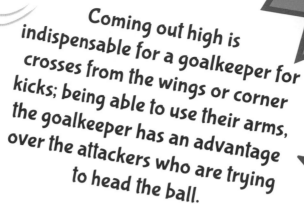

Coming out high is indispensable for a goalkeeper for crosses from the wings or corner kicks; being able to use their arms, the goalkeeper has an advantage over the attackers who are trying to head the ball.

THE CATCH

If the ball is coming at height and with a predictable trajectory, we can try to catch it in our hands. This is a technique that gives confidence to the goalkeeper and the whole defense, but it has to be done safely in order to avoid a mistake becoming an assist for the opponents. Therefore, almost all goalkeepers catch the ball only if they are able to create space to take at least two steps running and are protected from the charge of the opposing strikers.

THE SECRET:

use the technique of the running jump, so that one knee is raised and acts as a shield against the attacker's charge; use both hands with the thumbs touching to prevent the ball from slipping out of the grip between the two gloves.

THE PARRY

When the ball comes at height, but the trajectory is not predictable or it is too fast, then we parry it with the fists. The movement is the same as coming out high: look for space to run two steps and jump with the knee high to gain momentum and keep opponents at a distance. But instead of trying to catch it, go towards the ball with the fists closed to knock it as far away as possible. If the trajectory allows, we use both fists together, otherwise we use one arm and protect ourselves and keep our balance with the other.

THE SECRET:

to give more force to the parry, it is necessary to give power to the arms by bending them before stretching them on impact; the body has to be frontally directed towards the ball.

THROWING AND KICKING

When we regain possession of the ball, we have to restart our team's attack.
To speed up the action, we can launch the ball using the hands or feet. Sometimes, we can surprise our opponents with a long delivery.

The long delivery allows us to reach a free teammate even at considerable distances. A well-trained goalkeeper can easily reach the opposing penalty area with a kick; with their hands, they can easily reach the center of the pitch. Kicking the ball involves lifting it with one hand and striking it in midair, before it touches the ground, with the instep. The technique with the hands is the same as that used in throwing the discus: prepare for the movement, then extend the arm rapidly in a circular motion.

THE SECRET:

use the wrist and fingers to give the ball a reverse spin that increases the length of the throw; if kicking, pull the leg kicking back while the ball is in flight.

In modern soccer, the goalkeeper takes part in the construction of the game, either launching the ball quickly and a distance away, or passing it short, as a back-up to the defenders at the start of the action.

THE LONG KICK

The long kick is used to deliver the ball directly to the attacking players, usually in a position in the middle of the opposing team's half. It is therefore a matter of kicking the ball with power and precision, often one-touch, that is, without stopping it, in order not to risk being pressured by opponents, sometimes following a pass back from a teammate. So it will be necessary to use the instep and, to increase the range of the kick, it is possible to give it a reverse spin, that is, an effect that also makes the bounce on the ground easier to control.

THE SECRET:

give power to the kicking leg by pulling it backwards, so that the pendulum movement is as wide as possible; to give the ball a reverse spin it is necessary to strike it in the lower part, stretching the toe of the foot beneath the ball.

THE SHORT PASS

Increasingly often teammates, perhaps because under pressure from the opposition strikers, try a back pass. In this case, the goalkeeper has to decide whether to kick the ball a long distance away or pass short to a teammate who is free. This solution is safer for the team and often allows them to start a planned and threatening move. The short pass does not need to be powerful but precise, preferably one-touch. Therefore, the side of the foot is usually used.

TEAM TECHNIQUES

Once individual technique has been learned, we have to remember that to play soccer well, we are part of a group. So there is also a team technique that we need to know and practice. The basics of team technique are man-to-man and zone marking, the use of pressure, and the use of offside.

Sweeper

MAN MARKING

When the ball is with the opposing team, we have to stop them scoring goals and recover the ball as quickly as possible. How? In modern soccer there is a tendency to distinguish between man-to-man defense and zone defense: the first is based on controlling the opponent, the second on controlling the zone of competence.

THE DUEL

Man marking involves a number of one-on-one duels around the field of play: each player has an opponent to control and never let out of their sight. As a result these pairings are maintained in both attack and defense. The duel is fascinating, but dangerous; if the attacker gets past the defender, they will have a free run towards the goal!

THE SWEEPER

For this reason, man defense involves a kind of life-saver: the sweeper. They are the only player free from marking tasks and therefore available to block any gaps that appear in our defense. Usually they are positioned slightly behind the last defender.

THE HALFBACK

To help the sweeper, man-to-man defense also includes the halfback; they play in midfield and are mainly dedicated to defense, marking the most advanced opposition midfielder but also keeping an eye open for any incoming threats. Having to do twice the work, the halfback has a lot of running to do!

HOW TO MAN MARK

There are five basic rules for man marking:

1 If we are very close to the opponent we will be a nuisance to them, but run the risk of not having enough time to react to what they do. For this reason, usually, the closer the opponent comes to our goal (or the ball), the tighter the marking becomes, but if the opponent is a distance away from the ball or the goal, the marking is less tight.

2 Since, if we are passed, an immediate threat is created, we try not to enter into a tackle if we are not sure of winning the ball or at least delaying the opponent's action. It is best to accompany them as a screen and put them off.

3 We must never lose sight of our opponent, but we have to also follow the action to try to figure out whether the ball is going to come to us. The ideal would be to have four eyes, but since this is not possible, we use our arms and body to maintain contact, especially in the area (but being careful not to commit a foul!).

4 We have to use the space created between the feet and the ball whenever the opponent controls it. In the same way, we have to learn to insert ourselves in the space between the ball and the opponent's body. By doing this, we put pressure on them and reduce their sense of security.

5 We ask for and provide help to our teammates; it is almost impossible to stay focused throughout the game without our opponent getting away from us at least once!

HOW TO ESCAPE MAN MARKING

If we have possession of the ball and the opponent is man marking us, we will soon start to become nervous... To escape man marking there are some tricks we can use:

➤ it is easier to get away from the control of a defender if we do not have the ball at our feet, also because in addition to our movements, the opponent will have to follow those of the ball;

➤ pretend to go towards the ball and race off in the opposite directions; this serves to disorient the defender and make them uncertain about what we are planning;

➤ we go to meet the ball, so we do not allow the defender to get there before us when we receive a pass;

➤ if we have our back to the goal, we defend the ball using our body as a barrier, then lean on the opponent, using our arms as well; when we decide to move, they will not have the space and time to react and will find themselves running after us.

ZONE MARKING

COVERING

When an opponent comes at us and gets past us, our defense is likely to be under threat. But zone defense foresees the cover of another defender in our zone to cover the gap opened up by the opponent. With an organized covering system, if a player on our team is passed, everyone moves like the pieces on a chessboard, going to provide cover where it is needed. Obviously, this organization cannot be improvised and the movements need to be practiced in training.

Zone defense requires each player to control a part of the pitch, regardless of the opponent in front of them. Thus the team occupies the space in a broader and more complete way; thanks to the covering and the diagonal, if an opponent gets past our defender, they immediately find themselves facing another defender.

The defect of this system is that sometimes it leaves too much room to the opponent, especially in the penalty area; in addition, in order to work well, the zone requires a notable collective organization and extensive collaboration between teammates.

DIAGONAL

The diagonal is perhaps the most common covering movement in the game. It happens when, for example, a wing defender is passed: one of the two central defenders runs to the side to oppose the attacker but, in this way, a gap opens in the center of the area that is closed thanks to the other wing defender moving to the center. This is the defensive diagonal.

DOUBLE DEFENDING

To help a player in difficulty, zone defense employs double defending; it is usually the teammate in the adjacent zone who approaches to make dribbling or passing for the opponent more difficult. To work well, double defending involves a continuous system of covering, so that no area close to the one where the ball is remains uncovered.

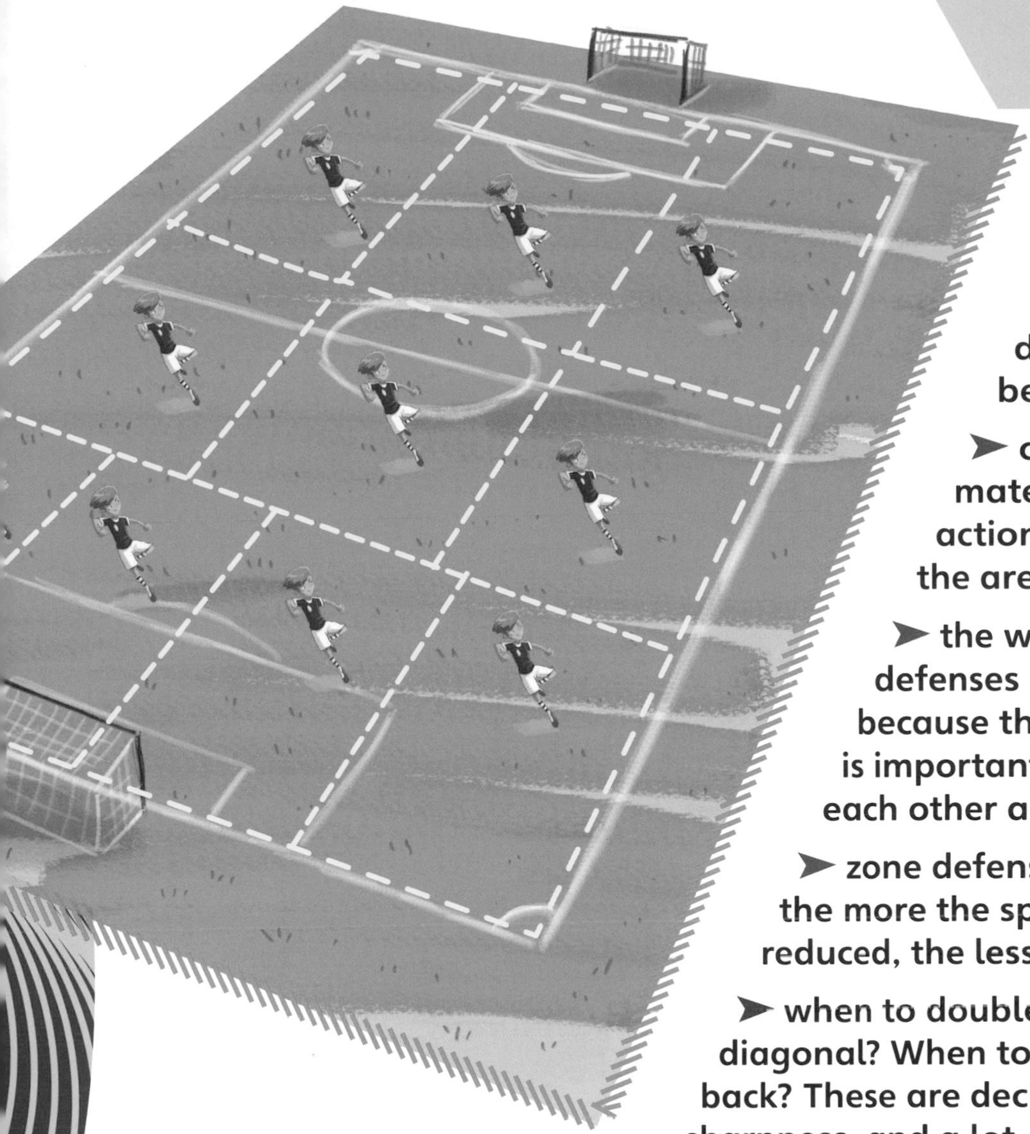

HOW TO ZONE MARK

The zone defense requires some special attention:

➤ double defending, that is, helping the teammate in difficulty, reduces the risk of them being passed;

➤ covering in the area of our team-mate must be a collective and chain action; if only the closest player moves, the area they occupied remains empty;

➤ the weak point of almost all zone defenses is the center of the defensive line, because there is no sweeper. Therefore it is important for the defenders to talk with each other a lot and be organized;

➤ zone defense reasons in terms of space: the more the space available to the attackers is reduced, the less danger there will be;

➤ when to double defend, cover, and use the diagonal? When to apply pressure? When to pull back? These are decisions that require organization, sharpness, and a lot of thought.

HOW TO ATTACK A ZONE DEFENSE

Zone defense also has its defects. A good attack has to try to exploit them:

➤ this type of defense brings many players around the ball; in doing so, there are zones of the pitch that remain free. A good attack sees these areas and moves the ball to send it there;

➤ missing the sweeper, the zone defense plays with the central defenders in a line. Strikers can take advantage of this feature by just staying onside or attempting to dribble through the middle;

➤ a zone defense tends to be drawn forward. A well-organized team can overcome it with passes over the defensive line;

➤ zone defense requires collective and synchronized movements. The attacking team can put this organization under pressure with an intense series of passes, which forces the other team to adjust its balance, and passing the ball horizontally and vertically to make the defenders move and lose their distances.

PRESSURE

Applying pressure, that is, playing aggressively against the opponent when they are in possession of the ball, was not invented in the era of modern soccer; there have always been soccer players who, thanks to personal traits, specialized in the quick recovery of the ball by attacking the opponent. But pressure applied as a team activity has been adopted in relatively recent times.

CROWDING OUT

Applying pressure means, in short, stealing from the person in possession the space to move and to pass, and the time to choose what to do. In soccer slang it is called crowding out. The player in possession of the ball has to have the impression of being completely surrounded...

PSYCHOLOGICAL WAR

The team being pressured risks finding itself in great difficulty; whoever has the ball is attacked and, struggling to find a free teammate, is obliged to try a tricky dribble or a pointless long kick. This is one of the most important goals of applying pressure: to remove the opponent's feeling of security and win the psychological war.

THE OBJECTIVES

The team that does not have possession of the ball attacks the opponents for five reasons:

➤ to reduce the space available to those setting the game;

➤ to limit the time available to those setting the game;

➤ to increase the likelihood of a mistake in passing or dribbling;

➤ to recover the ball near the opposing goal and so increase the threat of the attack;

➤ to psychologically condition the opponent.

THE COUNTERATTACK

Pressure, if properly applied, leads to the retrieval of the ball. And then? The team that recovers the ball finds itself in the best position to attack their opponents who are now off balance: in modern soccer this is called the counterattack.

HOW TO APPLY PRESSURE

Applying pressure is a very profitable way of defending, but can also be quite dangerous; if it is done badly, it offers opponents more advantages than difficulties. Here are some recommendations, for both team and individual players:

➤ if man marking, applying pressure is riskier; to do one-against-one it is necessary to give up the sweeper and so uncover the center of the defense;

➤ if zone marking, applying pressure is the natural consequence of the organization of the defensive system; with the defense in a line and with the habit of double defending and covering, it is easy to move the whole team forward and crowd out around the ball;

➤ the keys to applying pressure are in fact the same as zone defense: helping the partner, double defending, the diagonal, and crowding out. From this it can be understood that a well-applied pressure is organized and collective, involving all the players in an intelligent way;

➤ never apply pressure alone; it is a waste of energy and only helps the opponent;

➤ without decisiveness and aggressiveness, applying pressure risks being pointless.

HOW TO ESCAPE PRESSURE

If our opponents are good at applying pressure, we will gradually find ourselves playing without the ball, always in defense and with our morale low. So we have to find countermeasures. Here is what we can do when we have the ball:

➤ use the goalkeeper as back-up when the opposing pressure pushes us close to our area. But after giving the ball to the goalkeeper, move in such a way as to be free to receive the return pass; otherwise the goalkeeper will be forced to kick long;

➤ resort to dribbling only as a last resort; if the pressure is well organized, after beating the first opponent we will immediately find a second and then a third and we will lose the ball;

➤ look to teammates for help; the less we hold the ball at our feet, the less of an easy target we are;

➤ it is not possible to escape pressure without running; so we need to forget about being lazy and keep moving all the time, to force the opponent to run after us and give our teammates the chance to find at least one free player;

➤ if we have a strong physical attacker who is good at protecting the ball, we can overcome the pressure with a long pass. Our teammate will have to stop the ball, defend it for the time it takes to get the team up, and find a free player to pass to.

THE USE OF OFFSIDE

Starting in the 1970s, a number of teams (for example, Cruyff's Ajax) began to use what was called the offside tactic: advancing the line of defenders before a pass, to leave the attackers offside.

An intelligent and not very tiring way to recover the ball! Provided the move is done well, the defending players need to talk a lot and move all together.

The rule

A player is offside, in the opposing team's half, if they start beyond the last defender to receive a pass. What counts, then, is the position at the time of the pass, not when they receive the ball.

WHO CONTROLS THE DEFENSE

To use the offside rule to our advantage, we have to organize our defense so that everyone moves forward at the same time.

BUT WHEN TO MOVE? Almost all defenses have a player who commands the moves, shouts instructions to teammates, and decides the timing.

THE SHORT TEAM

Advancing the line of defenders can provide us with various advantages. In addition to putting the opponents in an offside position, we keep the team short, that is, we ensure there is a reduced distance between the furthest-back defender and the most-forward attacker. In this space, therefore, there are many players, who create a crowd and make the game difficult for opponents.

COVERED AND UNCOVERED BALL

A criterion for deciding whether to apply the offside tactic is what is called covered and uncovered ball. We say covered ball when the attacking team is in a moment of difficulty; for example when pressure is being applied on them, the player in possession of the ball is facing the other way, or lots of players are out of position. Instead we say uncovered ball when the player in possession of the ball has time and space to evaluate the game well and his teammates are well positioned. In the first case, the defending team can move the line without running too many risks; in the second case it would be better to wait.

HOW TO USE OFFSIDE

To use the offside tactic well, we have to pay attention to certain aspects of the game:

➤ we have to decide who controls the line of defenders and tells them to move forward; they have to be good at seeing if the ball is covered or uncovered;

➤ we have to practice positioning and movements a lot;

➤ we have to ask the whole team to help: for example by applying pressure, to put the person with the ball in difficulty;

➤ we have to give up man marking; the offside tactic requires a collective organization that goes better with zone defense;

➤ we have to have a plan B in case the opponents employ countermeasures. Usually, the plan B consists of a fast player who runs back to cover the ball if needed;

➤ the goalkeeper has to play very high, often in the penalty area semicircle, in order to be able to intervene with a long kick like a defender.

HOW TO PLAY AGAINST THE OFFSIDE TACTIC

The team that uses offside tactics accepts they are taking a risk. We have to use the weak points of the tactic to attack them:

➤ if the defenders are not perfectly aligned, the movement might leave room for an attacker to enter;

➤ if the defenders are too slow moving forward, the attackers might come back from an offside position and move forward again, catching the defense unprepared;

➤ if the line of defense is too high, a space opens up between the last defender and the goalkeeper; with a well-placed deep pass it is possible to serve our players more quickly, if they move at the right time;

➤ sometimes patience is required: if we are under pressure and the opposing defense moves out well, we are in a covered ball moment which we can get out of by turning the action to find a free man who restarts the action with an uncovered ball.

TACTICS

Tactics are the way players line up on the field of play: the number of players per area, how they are placed, and how they move. There is an infinite number of formations, which change depending on the players and their characteristics.

THE HISTORICAL FORMATIONS

At the beginning of the history of soccer, formations, that is, the way the players line up on the pitch, did not exist; tactics were simple and not studied in much detail. In the earliest games it was not unusual to see teams organized in a 1-1-8 formation, that is, one defender, one midfielder, and eight strikers (or the more cautious 2-2-6...). At the end of the nineteenth century, teams started to organize themselves. From that moment, the historical formations were born.

THE 2-3-5, THE CAMBRIDGE PYRAMID

Until the 1930s, one of the most popular tactics in soccer was the Cambridge Pyramid, that is, 2-3-5. The formation was created by the British university team; it was then used by Blackburn Rovers, who, thanks to this formation, won five FA cups.

THE WW METHOD

The WW method was born from the evolution of the Pyramid. The creators of this formation were the Italian Vittorio Pozzo and the Austrian Hugo Meisl. With this method, Pozzo led Italy to two World Cup victories. There were four defenders: two central and two on the wings, assisted by a midfielder pulled back, the center-half, who was also the playmaker from the back of the team. Two attacking midfielders and three attackers completed the 2-3-2-3, or WW.

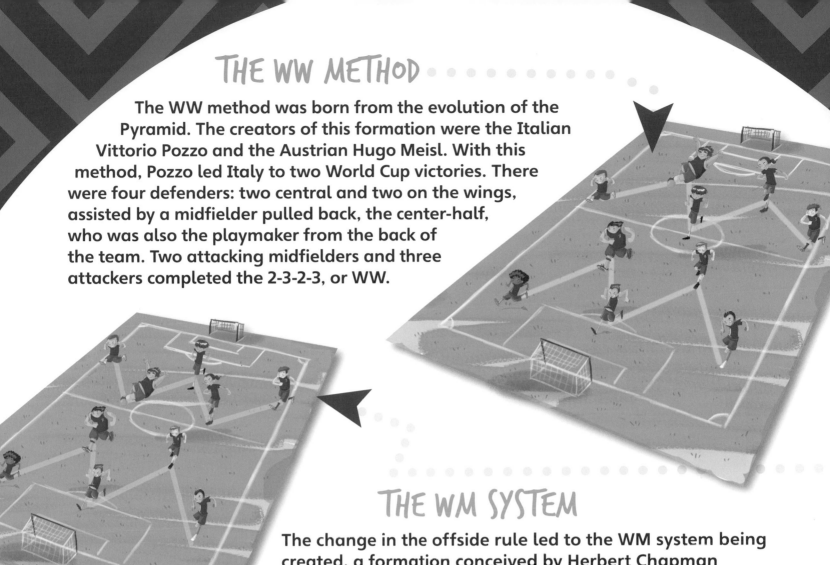

THE WM SYSTEM

The change in the offside rule led to the WM system being created, a formation conceived by Herbert Chapman (manager of Arsenal). He increased the number of defenders, with a center-half who had the task of marking the opposing center forward. The four midfielders were arranged in a quadrilateral: the two at the rear had defensive duties, the two at the front were in support of the three strikers. For many years, it was the most widely used way of playing in the world.

THE DANUBE MM

3-2-3-2, also referred to as MM (or Danube System), derives from the WM system and was developed by Gusztáv Sebes, the coach of Hungary in the 1950s. While the defense remained the same, the two midfielders were joined by two covering wingers and a striker pulled back, who was inserted behind the two other strikers, a tactic made specifically to create a crowded midfield and enhance the dribbling ability of the Hungarians.

DEFENSE ABOVE ALL

With the increase in the number of matches and international-level teams, from the 1930s, many games ended up with spectacular results and rich in goals. Players loved the open confrontation and did not organize themselves, so the strongest teams easily won the individual duels and therefore the matches. In the 1930s, people began to think of formations that protected defenses more and reduced the gap between the richest teams and the poorer teams in terms of talent.

THE SWISS VERROU

In 1932, Karl Rappan, the Servette manager, decided to devise a formation that avoided his team being defeated all the time. The idea worked; it involved placing a player behind the three defenders, who were to mark the attacker. The last player was the sweeper, a defender with the role of the last man who had to close down any gaps that appeared in the defense.

CATENACCIO AND ZONA MISTA

Verrou changed the way of interpreting games from first of all score goals to first of all do not concede goals.
The evolution of Verrou occurred in the years that followed with catenaccio, which was used by almost all Italian teams between the 1950s and 1970s. Compared to Verrou, catenaccio introduced the attacking fullback (usually on the left) and the ala tornante (usually on the right). In the 1980s, catenaccio was transformed into the zona mista: in front of the sweeper, two man-marking defenders, while midfielders and left-backs controlled their own zone. The key figure was the defensive midfielder, a midfielder who protected the defense.

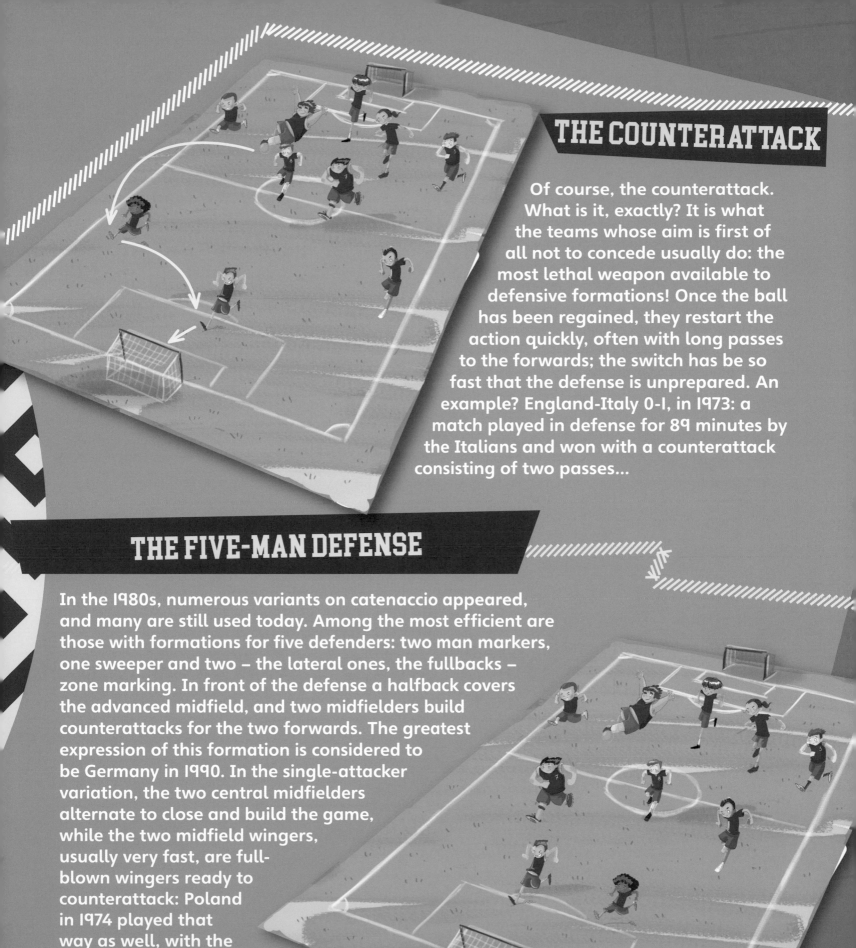

THE COUNTERATTACK

Of course, the counterattack. What is it, exactly? It is what the teams whose aim is first of all not to concede usually do: the most lethal weapon available to defensive formations! Once the ball has been regained, they restart the action quickly, often with long passes to the forwards; the switch has be so fast that the defense is unprepared. An example? England-Italy 0-1, in 1973: a match played in defense for 89 minutes by the Italians and won with a counterattack consisting of two passes...

THE FIVE-MAN DEFENSE

In the 1980s, numerous variants on catenaccio appeared, and many are still used today. Among the most efficient are those with formations for five defenders: two man markers, one sweeper and two – the lateral ones, the fullbacks – zone marking. In front of the defense a halfback covers the advanced midfield, and two midfielders build counterattacks for the two forwards. The greatest expression of this formation is considered to be Germany in 1990. In the single-attacker variation, the two central midfielders alternate to close and build the game, while the two midfield wingers, usually very fast, are full-blown wingers ready to counterattack: Poland in 1974 played that way as well, with the central striker acting as a center forward playing deep.

FORMATIONS WITH 4 DEFENDERS

The various modifications to the historical formations led to the emergence of numerous systems of play, which are still used. In general, there are systems with four and three defenders. The first are more numerous and have the most variants.

4-4-2 AND 4-4-1-1

With the four defenders in a line, four midfielders and two strikers, zone defense found its maximum expression. The 4-4-2 was the trademark of many leading English teams such as Liverpool, Nottingham Forest, and Aston Villa, who dominated Europe between 1976 and 1982, and the AC Milan of Arrigo Sacchi and the great Dutch players. 4-4-2 allows a coverage of the zones of play that is balanced and complete. In the single-striker version, there is an attacking midfielder behind them to increase the unpredictability for the lines of the opposition defense.

4-3-3 AND 4-5-1

4-3-3 and 4-5-1 are similar formations in their defensive setting (the two wingers form part of the midfield) but differ in attack. The two wingers of the first formation are more attacking, good at dribbling and heading for goal. The two midfield wingers also aim for the area, while the two fullbacks often advance to cross. So 4-3-3 is a very attacking formation, which requires great attention; it is easy for the team to become unbalanced.

4-2-3-1

In 4-3-3 there is no room for a true quarterback; the two midfielders have to do a great deal of running and tackling. If, however, our team can count on a talented forward, two wingers, and a central striker, 4-2-3-1 provides a good balance: behind the attacking players are two central midfielders, good in defense and in setting the tempo of the game.

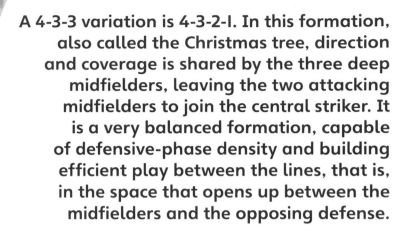

A 4-3-3 variation is 4-3-2-I. In this formation, also called the Christmas tree, direction and coverage is shared by the three deep midfielders, leaving the two attacking midfielders to join the central striker. It is a very balanced formation, capable of defensive-phase density and building efficient play between the lines, that is, in the space that opens up between the midfielders and the opposing defense.

4-2-4

This is the system adopted by Pelé's Brazil: four defenders, two of whom are fullbacks who often attack, two midfielders who run the game, two wingers who are very good at dribbling, and two central strikers. A very attacking formation, this system is only sustainable by teams that are attacking for the whole game and have particularly good players to overcome their opponents and score goals.

4-3-1-2 DIAMOND

An alternative to 4-3-2-I, this is a bit more attack-minded and involves the use of two strikers, who are served by a talented attacking midfielder, usually good at getting past the opposition and assisting. The three midfielders share the defensive and playmaking roles: the central one builds the game and stays in front of the defensive line, while one (or both) of the outside midfielders and one of the fullbacks come forward to assist in attacking play.

FORMATIONS WITH 3 DEFENDERS

Formations with three defenders are the descendents of highly ductile tactics such as the WM system and the Danube formation: three defenders allow better coverage at the back and permit the midfield to devote themselves to a very flexible defense and building job. For this reason, with only small modifications, the three-defender formations can be very defensive or very attacking.

3-4-3

This is a very attacking formation, which usually involves five or six players going forward. The player at the center of the three-man defense occupies the key role; in practice he replaces one of the two central defenders as needed and is also the first player to set up the action. Of the four midfielders, the two in the middle have covering and directing roles, but the two midfield wingers are decisive, because they have to defend fullbacks and attack as extra wingers, running up and down the touchline for miles.

3-3-4

3-3-4 is a formation inspired by the WW method. In the international field, with a number of variants, it was applied by Louis van Gaal (Ajax) and Marcelo Bielsa (Argentina and Chile). 3-3-4 is very aggressive: it involves two central strikers, playing close to each other, flanked by two wingers who play at the height of the forwards. When the wingers also have covering duties, the 3-3-4 looks much like 3-5-2. In this formation the four strikers are therefore decisive; they have to run a lot and attack but also help the team by applying pressure high on opposing defenders.

3-3-1-3

Cruyff (as a coach) and Van Gaal created the Ajax school of philosophy of the game, linked to 3-3-1-3, which is also related to the tiki-taka of Barcelona. This formation involves great movement on the pitch and, between roles, a continuous interchange that has to ensure the creation of spaces in the attack phase and balance between the covering players. The three defenders play a zone game, while the central midfielder is the playmaker and ready to cover in defense. The two wingers also have cover in the defensive phase, while the two strikers (one a little further forward) remain in the center. The players' athletic abilities are very important because this style of play is very tiring.

3-5-2

This is a formation which, depending on the players who interpret it, can be very aggressive or very defensive. Everything depends on three roles: the defensive center, who can be more or less predisposed to playmaking; the midfield center, who can be blocked in front of the defense or high up, in an attacking midfield position; and the two side players, who can be fullbacks, and are therefore more suitable to protecting the defense, or wingers, and are therefore strong in attack. One of its greatest expressions was provided by Carlos Bilardo of Argentina who used it at the 1986 World Cup, and went home victorious.

TOTAL SOCCER

Born in the 1970s, "total soccer" is a way of playing that includes the complete interchangeability of roles. Players in this system must be able to do everything: defend, apply pressure, attack. So, anyone who found themselves in the opposing area was able to score, and anyone who was found defending was able to do so. Even the goalkeeper was sometimes an added outfield player, capable of defending like a sweeper and establishing the tempo of the game like a midfielder.

THE PRINCIPLES OF DUTCH TOTAL SOCCER

In the early 1970s, Dutch teams dominated Europe by applying this revolutionary soccer tactic. At the 1974 World Cup, the Dutch national team brought this system to its highest level. Dutch total soccer involved:

1) Continuous movement without the ball
2) Applying pressure on the whole field of play
3) Interchangeability of roles
4) Zone marking
5) Offside tactic
6) Short squad
7) Exceptional (for the time) athletic preparation of the players

The main consequence of the Dutch model was the disappearance of the hyper-specialized player, and the emergence of the "total" soccer player, fast and resilient, able to move quickly in the various zones of the pitch and adapt to playing all roles.

THE PROPHET OF TOTAL SOCCER

In every game, Dutch star Johan Cruyff, though usually deployed as a center-forward, moved all over the field, depending on the development of the single actions, always looking for the position where he could be most dangerous. His teammates adapted their movements to his, exchanging positions regularly so that the roles were all covered, though not always by the same person.

3-1-3-1-2 FORMATION

This is the formation used by Ajax and Holland from the early 1970s. Each player had a starting position, but during the match they covered various other roles. In front of the goalkeeper there was only one true defender; the other two outside defenders were actually more inclined to attack than defend; the attacking midfielder could assist the defense, as well as setting the tempo or going for goal; the two outside midfielders could replace the fullbacks or move along the wings; the two forwards could go back to help the defense, back up the midfielders, or get into the area to finish the action. But the heart of the game was the two ones of the formation: the deep midfielder, who could play as sweeper and playmaker, increasing the number of defenders or midfielders as needed; and the deep striker, a player capable of starting the action everywhere, moving without the ball, or going to finish a move, maybe after dribbling past his marker.

TIKI-TAKA

Tiki–taka is a way of playing based on a long series of short passes intended to keep possession of the ball. The aim is to decrease the opportunities and time available to the opponent to do anything, forcing them to pursue the ball and tire themselves out. It is a way of playing that finds its historical inspiration in the Danube system and in Dutch total soccer (its closest relative). But compared to total soccer, it needs more technique and less physical strength.

THE BEST DEFENSE IS ATTACK

Tiki-taka involves a continuous exchange of position between midfielders, defenders, and strikers; in fact, a real division of roles does not exist because, by always being in possession of the ball, those who play tiki-taka have no need to go from defending to attacking. Tiki-taka allows a team to defend simply by holding the ball and not marking your opponents, so that the other team is forced to run around to try to win the ball.

THE FALSE NINE

Teams that adopt tiki-taka often play 4-6-0 or 3-7-I. But we must remember that this is more of a tactical attitude than a proper formation, because, as has been said about teams that are good at passing, "the ideal is a group of eleven midfielders." Even the central striker is in fact an attacking midfielder, hence the name "false nine," (i.e., false center forward), who is consistently involved both in building the attack directly and in opening spaces for the midfielders and wingers to come in. The most famous example is Messi in Guardiola's Barcelona.

BARCELONA AND SPAIN

Guardiola's Barcelona and Spain, who won everything between 2008 and 2012, are the teams that brought tiki-taka to the fore.
Both formations started from a theoretical 4-3-3, but on the pitch the division of roles was invisible, as almost all the players were interchangeable. Barcelona, in particular, was the extreme version of the tiki-taka: a team made up of only midfielders! After all, Javier Mascherano, Sergio Busquets, and Gerard Piqué were midfielders, even if used in defense; and Xavi, Iniesta, and Fàbregas were midfielders, even if used in attack...

10 EASY EXERCISES to start PLAYING

PASSING THE BALL

This exercise is for two players, standing in front of each other, about 6 to 10 feet apart. The first ball is kicked along the ground, slowly at first, then progressively harder; whoever receives it must strike it on the volley, that is, without stopping it, and send it back to their teammate. Alternate between the feet and way of kicking; from close up, strike the ball with the side of the foot, as the distance increases, hit it with inside or the instep.

HEADING THE BALL

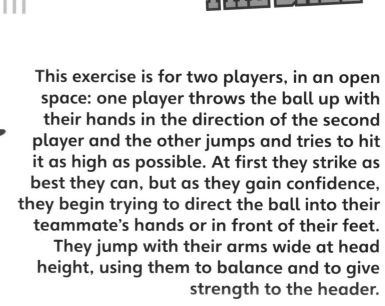

This exercise is for two players, in an open space: one player throws the ball up with their hands in the direction of the second player and the other jumps and tries to hit it as high as possible. At first they strike as best they can, but as they gain confidence, they begin trying to direct the ball into their teammate's hands or in front of their feet. They jump with their arms wide at head height, using them to balance and to give strength to the header.

CONTROLLING THE BALL IN TRAFFIC

Two groups face each other, about 30 feet apart. Each player has their ball at their feet and travels forward with it, first walking and then increasing the pace. The two groups meet halfway and have to keep control of the ball in the confusion that is created. They arrive at the starting point of the opposite group, turn around, and start again.

BOUNCING

The player starts with their preferred foot to try to hold the ball up as long as possible. Then they do the same with their nondominant foot. Finally, they try to make as many bounces of the ball as possible by alternating their feet. The ball is bounced on the instep of the foot, so the ankle must be very stiff when impact with the ball occurs. The supporting leg has to be slightly bent, the arms wide to keep balance.

DRIBBLING

With the ball at their feet, players slalom between a row of cones. They begin with the right foot, using both the inside of the foot and the outside; then repeat the exercise with the left foot. The ball must be as close to the foot as possible; the arms should be wide to maintain the best balance during changes of direction. The first slaloms will be slow, then gradually accelerate, trying to take less and less time to complete the whole path.

STOPPING WITH THE FOOT

This exercise is for two players, facing each other, about 16 feet apart. One throws the ball with their hands, sometimes high, sometimes low; the other has to stop the ball with one foot and return it with the other foot. Depending how the ball arrives, they will try to stop it with the instep or side of the foot. The aim is to keep it at a reduced distance, so it can be kicked back without making any further movements.

STOPPING WITH THE CHEST

This exercise is for two players, facing each other, about 10 feet apart. One player throws the ball up with their hands in the direction of the second player; the other looks for it so that it bounces on the top of their chest and then drops nearby. The aim is to kick it back to the teammate. The arms should be kept wide to improve balance and take aim. Bending the legs a little and deflating the chest at impact will allow the ball to fall to the ground near the feet.

SHOOTING AT GOAL

Players stand just in front of the goal, about 6 feet from a cone. With the ball at their feet, players begin to pass the cone by moving the ball to the right, and shoot immediately, aiming the shot at the post on the left. The ball is recovered, and the exercise is repeated moving left and shooting left-footed at the right post. The ball should be hit with the instep or inside of the foot, with the greatest possible force.

GOING FOR THE BALL (KEEP AWAY)

This exercise requires at least four players: three form a triangle, about 16 feet from each other, while the fourth goes to the center. The three players pass the ball, trying not to be intercepted, ideally using one-touch passes; the player in the middle tries to touch it, applying pressure to the player with the ball and trying to understand the lines of the pass. If they succeed, they take the place of the teammate who attempted the last pass.

DEFENDING THE BALL

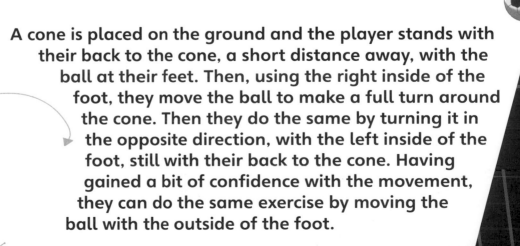

A cone is placed on the ground and the player stands with their back to the cone, a short distance away, with the ball at their feet. Then, using the right inside of the foot, they move the ball to make a full turn around the cone. Then they do the same by turning it in the opposite direction, with the left inside of the foot, still with their back to the cone. Having gained a bit of confidence with the movement, they can do the same exercise by moving the ball with the outside of the foot.

5 EASY EXERCISES to start to PLAY

GOALKEEPER

DIVING

To learn how to dive to the side, it is necessary to get used to lowering the legs a lot, keeping them fairly wide; then flexing a little, shifting the weight from the left to the right leg and vice versa.
To dive to the right, the right leg is folded and the left is extended. During the first exercises simply fall, using the bent right arm to dampen the blow; a little at a time, move more forcefully, dropping ever farther away.

IMPROVING REFLEXES

This exercise requires at least four players: three form a triangle, about 16 feet from each other, while the fourth goes to the center. The three players pass the ball with their hands trying not to be intercepted; the player in the middle – the goalkeeper – tries to catch it, trying to understand the lines of the pass. If they succeed, they take the place of the teammate who made the last pass.

GETTING
HIGH BALLS

This exercise is for two players. One player throws the ball up with their hands in the direction of the second player; the other tries to grab it, jumping as high as possible. The player throwing the ball alternates chips with faster shots to surprise the player jumping. The latter should try to use a running jump, employing a minimum run-up and taking off with one foot, so as to raise one knee.

SAVING WITH
THE FEET

This exercise is for two players: the goalkeeper, at the edge of the area, and an outfield player, in the center of the pitch. The latter passes the ball backwards, at ground level. The goalkeeper goes to the ball and hits it first time, trying to kick it as far away as possible. With this exercise, the goalkeeper will be able to knock it exactly to their teammate's feet. The kick has to be made using the instep.

THROWING

This exercise is for two players standing about 33 feet apart. Facing each other, the two goalkeepers pass the ball by throwing it with one hand, using the rotation technique (the same used in throwing the discus). The more precise they become, the further apart they can move, so as to simulate the throw professional goalkeepers make. To do the movement well, they need to twist the trunk and use the arm that does not have the ball as leverage.

NATIONAL TEAMS

National soccer teams, (i.e., those representing countries) began to meet officially at the Olympics, starting in 1900. But some friendly matches and one tournament – the British Home Championship, played between the national teams of England, Wales, Scotland, and Ireland (later Northern Ireland) – began in 1883. From that moment, international matches became the most important and entertaining in competitive soccer.

THE WORLD CUP

The FIFA World Cup, which is held every four years, is the most important competition in world soccer. It was conceived in 1930 by Jules Rimet, the then-president of FIFA. The actual Rimet Cup was awarded to Brazil in perpetuity, when they won it for the third time. The World Cup at present is contested by 32 teams (though this will become 48), selected through qualifying rounds in the 2 years prior to the finals. Eight countries have won at least one World Cup: Brazil (5 wins), Italy and Germany (4), Argentina, Uruguay, and France (2), and England and Spain (1).

THE EUROPEAN CHAMPIONSHIPS

The European Soccer Championships is a tournament that takes place every four years, midway between World Cups, and brings together the best European national sides. Since 2016 the finals have been contested by 24 teams. The trophy has so far been won by ten countries: Germany and Spain (3), France (2), and Czechoslovakia, Denmark, Greece, Italy, Holland, Portugal, and the Soviet Union (1).

THE COPA AMÉRICA

This is contested every four years by the South American countries (as well as two teams from other federations, usually from Central and North America). First held in Argentina in 1916, it is the oldest international event after the Olympics. In the 45 tournaments to date, eight countries have won the trophy: Uruguay (15), Argentina (14), Brazil (8), Chile, Paraguay, and Peru (2), and Bolivia and Colombia (1).

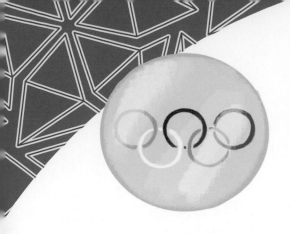

OLYMPIC GAMES

Soccer is among the disciplines that have almost always been practiced at the Summer Olympic Games and for many years it was also the only official international soccer competition. The countries that have won the Olympic tournament several times are Hungary and Great Britain (3), and Argentina, the Soviet Union, and Uruguay (2).

CONFEDERATIONS CUP

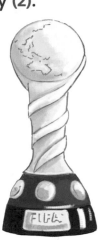

The FIFA Confederations Cup is played by the six champions of the continental federations, the reigning world champions, and the host country. It is played in the year preceding the FIFA World Cup in the same country that is going to host the World Cup. So far it has been won by Brazil (4), France (2), and Argentina, Mexico, and Denmark (1).

OCEANIAN NATIONS CUP

ASIAN CUP

CONCACAF GOLD CUP

AFRICA CUP OF NATIONS

THE OTHER CONTINENTAL CUPS

AOceania, Asia, Africa, and North-Central America also have continental international competitions. The Oceanian Nations Cup has so far been dominated by New Zealand (5 victories, followed by Australia with 4); the Asian Cup by Japan (4 wins, followed by Saudi Arabia with 3); the Africa Cup by Egypt (7 successes, followed by Cameroon with 5); and the CONCACAF Gold Cup by Mexico (10 wins, followed by the US with 5).

THE BALLON D'OR

The Ballon d'Or, which began life as the "European Soccer Player of the Year," is a soccer award established in 1956 by the French soccer magazine *France Football* and given each year to the best player in the world. The honor has been won by some of the most famous soccer players in history: Maradona, Cruyff, Platini, Beckenbauer, van Basten, Ronaldo... The past 10 years have seen an ongoing duel between Leo Messi and Cristiano Ronaldo.

FRANCE

1998 **2018** **1984** **2000**

The French national soccer team is one of the strongest in the world. They had their best periods in the 1980s when they won a European Championship (1984), and between the late 1990s and early 2000s when they won a World Cup (1998) and a European Championship (2000). France won the World Cup for a second time in 2018.

Among the great players who have worn the blue jersey are Michel Platini, the team's leader in the eighties, and Zinedine Zidane, a top midfielder in the early 2000s. Currently, the French national team is among the best in the world: Paul Pogba, Antoine Griezmann, Kylian Mbappé, N'Golo Kanté, Alexandre Lacazette, Olivier Giroud, and Dimitri Payet are some of their outstanding top players.

Michel PLATINI

Antoine GRIEZMANN

Paul POGBA

Zinedine ZIDANE

ITALY

1934   1938   1982   2006   1968

ITALIA
FIGC

The Italian national team is traditionally one of the most important in Europe and the world. They won two World Cups in the 1930s ('34 and '38), one European Championship in 1968, and two other World Cups in 1982 and 2006.

In general, they do well in tournaments, except in the black years immediately following the loss of the leading team of the 1940s, the Grande Torino, in a plane crash. Many greats have worn the blue jersey: among these everyone remembers Gigi Riva, Gianni Rivera, Sandro Mazzola, Paolo Rossi, Roberto Baggio, Paolo Maldini, and Francesco Totti. Among today's most famous Italian players are Gianluigi Buffon, Giorgio Chiellini, Leonardo Bonucci, and Daniele De Rossi.

Paolo ROSSI

Paolo MALDINI

Roberto BAGGIO

Gianluigi BUFFON

URUGUAY

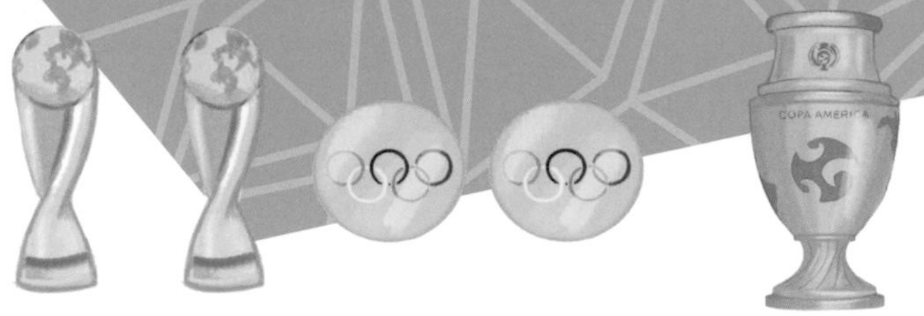

1930 **1950** **1924** **1928** 1916, 1917, 1920, 1923,
1924, 1926, 1935, 1942,
1956, 1959, 1967, 1983,
1987, 1995, 2011

The Uruguayan national side, known as "la Celeste," is one of the most prestigious nations historically. Uruguay is considered, along with Argentina and Brazil, to be the cradle of South American soccer. They were the first to organize and win a World Cup. Their great period was between the 1920s and 1950s, when they won two World Cups and two Olympic gold medals. They have won the Copa América 15 times.

Among the great players who have worn the sky-blue top are Nasazzi, Andrade, Schiaffino, Ghiggia, Mazurkiewicz, Francescoli, Fonseca, and Recoba. Currently their most famous soccer players are Diego Forlán, Edinson Cavani, Diego Godín, and Luis Suárez.

Juan Alberto
SCHIAFFINO

Edinson
CAVANI

Luis **SUÁREZ**

BRAZIL

1958　1962　1970　1994　2002　　2016　1919, 1922, 1949, 1989, 1997, 1999, 2004, 2007

CBF
BRASIL

The Brazilian national team, nicknamed "the Green and Yellow" from the color of their jerseys, is the most famous and prestigious national side in the world. They are the only nation to have participated in every World Cup, which they won five times. They have also won the Copa América eight times and an Olympic gold.

They are the interpreters of a way of playing enjoyable and spectacular soccer, which was renamed Futebol Bailado ("danced football," based on the Brazilian national dance: samba). Many champions have worn the green-and-yellow jersey, including Pelé, Garrincha, Zico, Sócrates, Falcão, Ronaldo, Roberto Carlos, and Ronaldinho. Among the most famous national players today are probably Kaká, Marcelo, Alves, Luiz, Silva, and Neymar.

RONALDO

NEYMAR

ZICO

PELÉ

THE NETHERLANDS

1988

The Dutch soccer team have earned their place in the history of soccer more for having changed the philosophy of the game than for what they have won. In fact, they have brought only one title home to Amsterdam: the 1988 European Championship. For the rest they have finished well in all competitions, reaching the final of the World Cup on three occasions. Their best times were between the 1970s and 1990s: in particular at the beginning of the 1970s, they revolutionized the way of playing, inventing so-called "total soccer" and earning the nickname of "Clockwork Orange." Among the great players who have worn the orange top are Cruyff, Neeskens, Gullit, van Basten, and Bergkamp. Currently their most famous soccerer is Arjen Robben.

Ruud GULLIT

Johan CRUYFF

Marco VAN BASTEN

Arjen ROBBEN

GERMANY

1954 1974 1990 2014

1972 1980 1996

Germany is, along with Italy, the most successful European nation in the history of soccer. First as West Germany, then as united Germany, they have won four World Cups and three European Championships (and East Germany, before unification, won the 1976 Olympics). They are also the nation that has reached the largest number of finals in the two major international competitions: eight times in the World Cup, and six in the European Championships.

Many stars have pulled on the white top, including Beckenbauer, Vogts, Gerd Müller, Overath, Netzer, Maier, Matthäus, Rummenigge, Völler, Sammer, and Kahn. Among the national players of today, the most famous are probably Neuer, Kroos, Özil, Götze, Khedira, and Thomas Müller.

Franz
BECKENBAUER

Thomas
MÜLLER

Manuel
NEUER

Karl-Heinz
RUMMENIGGE

RUSSIA

1960 1956 1988

Official heir to the Soviet Union's national soccer team, Russia has the largest number of participants in the sport in Europe and a top-notch technical tradition, although they have not won much in international competitions: a European Championship in the early 1960s, and two Olympic Games in 1956 and 1988. The former Soviet school changed the way of viewing soccer which, before the end of the 1970s, did not pay enough attention to the athletic element. Numerous stars have worn the red top of Russia-USSR: the most famous of all is probably Lev Jašin, one of the greatest goalkeepers of all time. In recent years, another goalkeeper Dasaev and two attackers Blochin and Zavarov have distinguished themselves.

Rinat DASAEV

Oleg BLOCHIN

Lev JAŠIN

HUNGARY

1952 1964 1968

Hungary is, in many people's memory, one of the most beautiful and unlucky national soccer teams in European history. Considered in the 1950s as a kind of invincible army, in its best decade it won only the 1952 Olympics. In 1954, they reached the World Cup final in Switzerland, but were stunned by West Germany. Nevertheless they put on a display of the finest soccer and invented a philosophy of play which took the name of "Danube soccer," based on control and short passes, a way of behaving on the pitch that closely resembled today's tiki-taka ... Among the greats who wore the red-green top, we remember Puskás, Hidegkuti, Albert, and, more recently, Nyilasi and Király.

Ferenc PUSKÁS

Tibor NYILASI

Gábor KIRÁLY

Flórián ALBERT

ARGENTINA

1978 **1986** 1921, 1925, 1927, 1929,
1937, 1941, 1945, 1946,
1947, 1955, 1957, 1959,
1991, 1993

2004 **2008**

Argentina is one of the most successful countries in the history of soccer since the early years of international competitions. They have won the World Cup twice, the Copa América 14 times, and the Olympics twice. On many other occasions the blue-and-white team have reached finals. In addition, they have given the world a large number of greats and the Argentine school continues to produce stars. Many famous players have worn white-and-blue-striped camisetta (top): Kempes, Passarella, Ardiles, Maradona, Valdano, Balbo, Verón, Batistuta, Zanetti, and Crespo... Among those playing today, the most famous names are those of Messi (Ballon d'Or winner on several occasions), Di María, Higuaín, Agüero, Dybala, Mascherano, and Tévez.

Leo MESSI

Mario KEMPES

Ángel DI MARÍA

Diego MARADONA

SPAIN

2010 2004 1964 2008 2012

The Curse of the World Cup lasted until 2010. Finally in South Africa, the Spanish national team managed to do what they had never achieved. Spain, in fact, has won the European Championship three times and the Olympics once, and have given European and world soccer great players and coaches. They also completed the longest winning run in European soccer, winning all the major competitions from 2008 to 2012, featuring the typical Spanish style tiki-taka. Among the champions wearing the red shirt of Spain, famous names stand out such as Zamora, Suárez, Gento, Butragueño, and Hierro, and more recently those of Casillas, Torres, Villa, Xavi, Ramos, Piqué, and Iniesta.

Sergio RAMOS

Andrés INIESTA

Emilio BUTRAGUEÑO

Luis SUÁREZ

ENGLAND

1966

ENGLAND

The English national soccer team, along with the Scottish, is the oldest in the world. For many years, the English, proud of this tradition and boasting of inventing modern soccer, did not participate in international competitions, except for the Olympics (twice won in 1908 and 1912, but with a British selection). In effect, the national soccer story begins with the 1950 World Cup. The first real satisfaction the English achieved was the 1966 World Cup, when they beat West Germany in the final. Since then, the results have been disappointing, far lower than the real value of English soccer. Many famous soccer players have pulled on the white top: Banks, Charlton, Keegan, Lineker, Beckham... Among the players still active the best-known names are those of Rooney, Gerrard, Lampard, and Sterling.

Wayne ROONEY

David BECKHAM

Bobby CHARLTON

Kevin KEEGAN

PORTUGAL

2016

Although rich in good players, in its history the Portuguese national team has not won much, despite often doing reasonably well, especially in the European Championships. Their only victory came in 2016, at the European Championships in France. It is no coincidence, however, that the best results in the history of Portugal have come when they had an unquestionable champion in their ranks, as when they won third place in the 1966 World Cup, thanks to the goals of Eusébio; or the victory of 2016, pursued ferociously by Cristiano Ronaldo, multiple Ballon d'Or winner. Sharing his fame today are the likes of Pepe, Quaresma, and Moutinho. Numerous other talents have worn the red shirt of Portugal. Among them, Futre, Sousa, Couto, Deco, and Figo are particularly famous.

Luís FIGO

EUSÉBIO

Cristiano RONALDO

POLAND

1972

In the World Cup, Poland came third in 1974 and 1982. They reached their first European Championship at Euro 2008 and made it to the quarterfinals of the tournament for the first time at Euro 2016. They won gold at the 1972 Olympics and silver in 1976 and 1992. The best years of Polish soccer are probably the 1970s and 1980s. Two generations of greats played in the white shirt; Tomaszewski, Kasperczak, Lato, Deyna, Zmuda, Szarmach, and Boniek... After 20 years of crisis, Polish soccer has again found a group of great players (Szczęsny, Zielinski, Milik, Linetty...) led by a great: Robert Lewandowski.

POLSKA

Grzegorz LATO

Arkadiusz MILIK

Robert LEWANDOWSKI

Zbigniew BONIEK

74

CZECH REPUBLIC

1976

FACR

Despite being able to count on top players, in its history the Czech national team have never won any international trophies, but have been placed well, especially in the European Championships. They were founded in 1993, at the same time as Slovakia, following the division of Czechoslovakia and the disappearance of the Czechoslovakian national team. They reached the final of the 1996 European Championship, where they were defeated by Germany, and the semifinal in 2004, where they lost to Greece. As Czechoslovakia, the red–blue national team won a European championship in 1976 and twice reached the final of the World Cup, in 1934 and 1962. Numerous talents have written their story: Masopust, Ondruš, Nehoda, Veselý, and Panenka... The names of Nedved, Koller, Baroš, Šmicer, Rosický, Berger, Jankulovski, Poborský, and Cech also stand out among the players of the Czech Republic.

Petr ČECH

Pavel NEDVĚD

Milan BAROŠ

CHINA

China's national soccer team has achieved their greatest successes in the Asian Cup, which they have never won, but came second in 1984 and in 2004 (when they hosted the competition), two third places in 1976 and 1992, and two fourth places in 1988 and 2000. They participated in only one World Cup, Japan–South Korea 2002. However, Chinese soccer is growing rapidly, due to substantial investments by major companies and the state, and thanks to the number of people practicing the sport, estimated to be over ten million. Numerous professional clubs play in the Super League, which was won for six consecutive years by Guangzhou Evergrande. Many top clubs have signed stars from European and South American championships such as Paulinho, Jackson Martinez, Hulk, Oscar, Pelè, and Witsel, or home-grown talent, such as Gao Lin, Zhang Linpeng, Wang Dalei, Wu Lei, and Zheng Zhi.

WU Lei

ZHENG Zhi

ZHANG Linpeng

GAO Lin

1991, 2002, 2005, 2007, 2013

The United States have won five CONCACAF Gold Cups (1991, 2002, 2005, 2007 and 2013) and have played in ten World Cups, where they came third in 1930 and reached the quarterfinals in 2002. The men's national team at the moment is less famous than the women's one, which is dominating the international scene having won three world championships (1991, 1999, and 2015), four Olympics (1996, 2004, 2008, and 2012), ten Algarve Cups, and seven CONCACAF Women's Gold Cups. At the national level, a large movement backed by almost ten million participants has created one of the richest leagues in the world, Major League Soccer, featuring many prominent soccerers such as Pirlo, Giovinco, Kaká, Villa, and Lampard... On the other hand, over the years, many American players have played in Europe: among them the best-known are Cobi Jones, Lalas, Bradley, Edu, Donovan, and Dempsey.

Maurice EDU

Clint DEMPSEY

Michael BRADLEY

Landon DONOVAN

FAMOUS CLUBS

The first club teams were born towards the end of the nineteenth century. At first, matches were friendlies and only in 1872 was the first official competition played, the FA Cup. In 1888, again in England, the first championship was established. More or less at the same time, the first international club competitions began, such as the Challenge International du Nord.

UEFA CHAMPIONS LEAGUE	UEFA EUROPA LEAGUE	COPA LIBERTADORES	CLUB WORLD CUP	NATIONAL CUPS	CUP WINNERS CUP	NATIONAL CHAMPIONSHIP	ASIAN CHAMPIONS LEAGUE

THE CHAMPIONS LEAGUE

The UEFA Champions League is the European competition that replaced the old European Cup, which was born in the 1950s and had been only for the teams that had won their respective national championships. Now up to four teams per nation might take part, depending on the importance of the championship. It is undoubtedly the most sought-after trophy for European clubs. The most successful team is Real Madrid (12 titles), followed by Milan (7), and Liverpool, Bayern Munich, and Barcelona (5).

THE EUROPA LEAGUE

The UEFA Europa League replaced the old UEFA Cup and Cup Winners Cup in 2009. The best teams from each European championship not playing in the Champions League take part. The team with the most wins is Seville (5), followed by Juventus, Inter, and Liverpool (3).

THE COPA LIBERTADORES

The Libertadores Cup is the principal South American club competition in soccer. The most successful team is Independiente (7 wins), followed by Boca Juniors (6) and Peñarol (5).

THE UEFA SUPER CUP

The UEFA Super Cup, commonly known as the European Super Cup, is a trophy contested by the winners of the Champions League and the Europa League. The clubs that have had their name inscribed most often on the trophy are Barcelona and AC Milan (5 each).

THE CLUB WORLD CUP

The Club World Cup is contested every year by the winners of the Champions Leagues of the various continents (plus the champions from the host country). It is the heir to the old Intercontinental Cup. Leading the list of teams that have won it the most is Real Madrid, which won three Intercontinental and two Club World Cups.

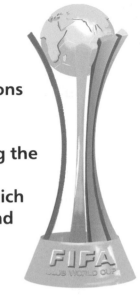

THE OTHER INTERNATIONAL CUPS

The European model of international cups has taken root on every continent. So now, there are the CONCACAF Champions League (for North, Central, and South America), the CAF Champions League (for Africa), the AFC Champions League (for Asia), and the OFC Champions League (for Oceania).

NATIONAL CHAMPIONSHIPS AND CUPS

Among the most famous championships are the Premier League (England), Bundesliga (Germany), Serie A (Italy), Liga (Spain), League (France), Primera División (Argentina), and Campeonato Brasileiro Série A (Brazil). In recent years, in terms of investment and number of stars, the Chinese (Super League), American (MLS), and Japanese (J1 League) championships have gained a great following. Among the world-famous national cups are the FA Cup (England), Copa del Rey (Spain), and Coupe de France (France).

THE GOLDEN BOOT

The Golden Boot is a prize given by UEFA to the player who, during the European soccer season, has scored most goals at club level. While at one time it was enough to score a lot of goals to win it, since 1997 to calculate the winner, it is necessary to multiply the number of goals scored in the league with the championship's coefficient of difficulty. Among those who have won it several times are Messi and Cristiano Ronaldo, who have won the prize four times each.

REAL MADRID

MADRID
(Spain)

Founding date: 1902
Stadium: Estadio Santiago Bernabéu (81,000 capacity)
Club colors: white
Stars: Di Stefano, Puskás, Gento, Raul, Butragueño, Santillana, Cristiano Ronaldo, Bale, Ramos, Benzema, Kroos, Modrić
Curiosity: holds the record for national trophies won, absolute primacy in European Cup/Champions League wins and, in general, in international titles won

BARCELONA

BARCELONA
(Spain)

Founding date: 1899
Stadium: Camp Nou (99,000 capacity)
Club colors: blue and burgundy
Stars: Cruyff, Maradona, Stoickov, Rivaldo, Ronaldinho, Guardiola, Puyol, Zamora, Zubizarreta, Xavi, Suárez, Neymar, Messi, Piqué, Busquets, Iniesta
Curiosity: the only European club team from 1955-56 to today to have always participated in at least one of the European cups

SEVILLE

SEVILLE
(Spain)

Founding date: 1890
Stadium: Estadio Ramón Sánchez-Pizjuán (43,000 capacity)
Club colors: white and red
Stars: Polster, Dasaev, Maradona, Zamorano, Ramos, Prosinečki, Rakitić, Llorente, Bacca
Curiosity: the oldest Spanish club dedicated exclusively to soccer and the only one to have won three consecutive Europa Leagues

ATLETICO MADRID

MADRID
(Spain)

Founding date: 1903
Stadium: Estadio Vicente Calderón (55,000 places)
From 2018: Wanda Metropolitan (67,000 capacity)
Club colors: white, red, and blue
Stars: Aragonés, Sánchez, Adelardo, Vieri, Forlán, Gabi, Torres, Griezmann, Villa, Agüero
Curiosity: Spain's third-placed soccer team in terms of titles won, and the only team that has won the Intercontinental Championship without ever having won the Champions League

AJAX

AMSTERDAM
(Netherlands)

Founding date: 1900
Stadium: Amsterdam Arena (54,000 capacity)
Club colors: white and red
Stars: Swart, Neeskens, Rep, Krol, Boer, Cruijff, van Basten, Michels, Suárez
Curiosity: the Dutch team has won the most trophies and is one of four clubs that have managed to win all three of the major European tournaments. In the 1970s, the Ajax of Rinus Michels invented so-called "total soccer"

PSV

EINDHOVEN
(Netherlands)

Founding date: 1913
Stadium: Philips Stadium (35,000 capacity)
Club colors: white and red
Stars: Koeman, Gerets, Lerby, Vanenburg, Wim Kieft, Cocu, Jonk, Stam, Van Nistelrooy, Van Bommel, Robben
Curiosity: PSV is one of the three great teams in the Netherlands along with Ajax and Feyenoord and is second in terms of trophies won

MILAN

MILAN
(Italy)

Founding date: 1899
Stadium: Meazza (80,000 capacity)
Club colors: red and black
Stars: Altafini, Rivera, Schiaffino, Liedholm, Cesare and Paolo Maldini, Nordahl, Baggio, Baresi, Gullit, Kaká, Rijkaard, Shevchenko, van Basten, Weah, Ibrahimovic, Pirlo
Curiosity: the third team in the world in terms of international trophies won (equal with Boca Juniors and behind Real Madrid and Al-Ahly)

CELTIC

GLASGOW
(Scotland)

Founding date: 1888
Stadium: Celtic Park (60,000 capacity)
Club colors: green and white
Stars: Johnstone, Lennox, Murdoch, Aitken, Dalglish, Larsson, Guidetti
Curiosity: Represents the Catholic part of Glasgow (the Protestants support Rangers). In 1967, Celtic became the first British club to win the European Cup

MANCHESTER UNITED

MANCHESTER
(England)

3   17   1   1   2   Premier 20

Founding date: 1878/1902
Stadium: Old Trafford (76,000 capacity)
Club colors: red, black, and white
Stars: Giggs, Charlton, Scholes, Neville, Rooney, Stepney, Dunne, Irwin, Spence, Law, Best, Giggs, Hughes, Van Nistelrooy, Ibrahimovic
Curiosity: One of the most famous teams in international soccer. They won their first European Cup in 1968, ten years after the plane crash that decimated the team

DINAMO KIEV

KIEV
(Ukraine)

20   2   Premier Liha 28

Founding date: 1927
Stadium: Olympic Stadium (70,000 capacity)
Club colors: blue and white
Stars: Blochin, Buryak, Rebrov, Yarmolenko, Shevchenko
Curiosity: the team of the former USSR and present-day Ukraine that won the most trophies. In the 1970s and 1980s, thanks to their coach Lobanovsky, they invented a sort of "socialist way" to total soccer

CHELSEA

LONDON
(England)

1   16   2   1   Premier 6

Founding date: 1905
Stadium: Stamford Bridge (42,000 capacity)
Club colors: royal blue
Stars: Wilkins, Gullit, Hughes, Wise, Zola, Di Matteo, Vialli, Cole, Terry, Frank, Essien, Drogba, Čech, Mata, Hazard
Curiosity: along with Juventus, Ajax, and Bayern Munich, one of the four clubs that have managed to win all three of the major European trophies

BORUSSIA DORTMUND

DORTMUND
(Germany)

1   4   1   1   Bundesliga 8

Founding date: 1909
Stadium: Westfalen Stadium (81,000 capacity)
Club colors: yellow and black
Stars: Sammer, Riedle, Chapuisat, Kohler, Zorc, Herrlich, Amorous, Lewandowski, Kagawa, Hummels, Götze
Curiosity: they have returned to the European elite after a period of crisis. In the 1990s, they won a Champions League, defeating Juventus in the final

BOCA JUNIORS

BUENOS AIRES
(Argentina)

 6 3 3 **I División**  32

Founding date: 1905
Stadium: EStadium Alberto J. Armando (La Bombonera) (49,000 capacity)
Club colors: yellow and blue
Stars: Gatti, Palermo, Riquelme, Maradona, Balbo, Batistuta, Caniggia, Verón, Tévez
Curiosity: the only Argentine team to never have been relegated and the third team in the world for the number of international trophies won

RIVER PLATE

BUENOS AIRES
(Argentina)

3 1 1 **I División** 36

Founding date: 1901
Stadium: Antonio Vespucio Liberti (El Monumental) (69,000 capacity)
Club colors: white and red
Stars: Di Stefano, Sivori, Fillol, Kempes, Francescoli, Díaz, Crespo
Curiosity: the club that won more titles in Argentina and the first team in Argentina to achieve the Triple Crown, winning the championship, the Libertadores Cup, and the Intercontinental Cup in the same season

SANTOS

SANTOS
(Brazil)

3 1 2 **Brasileirão** 30

Founding date: 1912
Stadium: Vila Belmiro (21,000 capacity)
Club colors: black and white
Stars: Pelé, Coutinho, Pepe, Zito, Serginho, Robinho, Neymar, Ganso
Curiosity: In the 1960s, Santos won, among other things, two Libertadores Cups and two Intercontinental Cups; the star of their successes was one of the all-time greats: Pelé

FLAMENGO

RIO DE JANEIRO
(Brazil)

 3 1 1 **Brasileirão** 39

Founding date: 1895
Stadium: Estádio da Gávea (official), or Estádio Maracanã (78,000 capacity)
Club colors: red and black
Stars: Gérson, Bebeto, Romário, Junior, Adriano, Garrincha, Sócrates
Curiosity: Flamengo is Brazil's most popular club, with an estimated 35 million fans, and is one of the most successful, with 39 championships, a Libertadores, and an Intercontinental Cup to their name

OLYMPIQUE MARSEILLES · PARIS ST. GERMAIN

MARSEILLE
(France)

PARIS
(France)

Ligue I

Ligue I

Founding date: 1899
Stadium: Stade Vélodrome (67,000 capacity)
Club colors: white and blue
Stars: Blanc, Deschamps, Dugarry, Pirès, Papin, Ribéry, Nasri, Drogba
Curiosity: in addition to being one of the most successful clubs in France in terms of trophies, they are the only French club to have been European champions, winning the Champions League in 1993

Founding date: 1904/1970
Stadium: Parc des Princes (48,000 capacity)
Club colors: blue, red, and white
Stars: Weah, Raí, Leonardo, Djorkaeff, Ginola, Lama, Giuly, Ronaldinho, Ménez, Maxwell, Lavezzi, Ibrahimović, Silva, Verratti, Cavani, Di María
Curiosity: born in 1970 from the merger between FC Paris and Stade St. Germain, PSG is, along with Marseilles, the team with the most fans in France

OLYMPIQUE LION · GUANGZHOU EVERGRANDE

LYON
(France)

CANTON
(China)

Ligue I

Super League

Founding date: 1950
Stadium: Parc Olympique Lyonnais (Parc OL) (59,000 capacity)
Club colors: white, blue, and red
Stars: Domenech, N'Gotty, Pelé, Amoros, Giuly, Juninho, Ben Arfa, Diarra, Malouda, Benzema, Coupet, Lloris, Lacazette, Gourcuff, Valbuena
Curiosity: in their history, Lyon won seven Ligue 1 championships consecutively (from 2001-2002 to 2007-2008)

Founding date: 1954
Stadium: Tianhe Stadium (60,000 capacity)
Club colors: red and white
Stars: Zhang Linpeng, Feng Xiaoting, Yang Jun, Jiang Ning, Yang Hao, Cléo, Conca, Diamanti, Gilardino, Paulinho, Martinez, Gao Lin, Zheng Zhi
Curiosity: the oldest Chinese club team and one of the most successful, they won six consecutive championships from 2011 to 2016

INTERNAZIONALE

MILAN
(Italy)

  3 7 3 3 Serie A 18

Founding date: 1902
Stadium: Meazza (80,000 capacity)
Club colors: black and blue
Stars: Suárez, Corso, Mazzola, Facchetti, Oriali, Bergomi, Rummenigge, Matthäus, Zenga, Ronaldo, Zanetti, Ibrahimović, Milito
Curiosity: one of the three Italian teams with most trophies and fans. In 2010 they achieved the treble, that is, the championship, the cup, and the Champions League

JUVENTUS

TURIN
(Italy)

 2 12 3 1 2 Serie A 33

Founding date: 1897
Stadium: Juventus Stadium (41,000 capacity)
Club colors: black and white
Stars: Boniperti, Sivori, Charles, Zoff, Platini, Scirea, Cabrini, Rossi, Baggio, Del Piero, Zidane, Nedvěd, Cannavaro, Buffon, Higuaín
Curiosity: the Italian team with the largest number of fans and the most successful in terms of national titles; they established a record of consecutive victories (6) between 2012 and 2017

BORUSSIA MÖNCHENGLADBACH

MÖNCHENGLADBACH
(Germany)

 3 2 Bundesliga 5

Founding date: 1900
Stadium: Stadium im Borussia-Park (54,000 capacity)
Club colors: white, green, and black
Stars: Netzer, Heynckes, Vogts, Simonsen, Wimmer, Bonhof, Kramer, Reus
Curiosity: one of the three most successful teams in Germany; had its best period in the 1970s when they won five championships, a German Cup, and two UEFA Cups

BAYERN

MUNICH
(Germany)

 5 24 1 1 3 Bundesliga 27

Founding date: 1900
Stadium: Allianz Arena (75,000 capacity)
Club colors: red, white, and blue
Stars: Maier, Beckenbauer, Gerd Müller, Breitner, Hoeness, Rummenigge, Matthäus, Klinsmann, Kahn, Schweinsteiger, Robben, Lahm, and Thomas Müller
Curiosity: the team that has won the most trophies in Germany and is also one of the most successful in the world, as well as the backbone of the German national team

PEÑAROL

MONTEVIDEO
(Uruguay)

5   3   I División 50

Founding date: 1891/1913
Stadium: Estadio Campeón del Siglo (41,000 capacity)
Club colors: yellow and black
Stars: Ghiggia, Schiaffino, Abbadie, Sansone, Varela, Máspoli, Cubilla, Mazurkiewicz, Forlán
Curiosity: the team in Uruguay with most trophies and among the few who have been able, on two occasions, to win the treble consisting of the national, continental, and world titles

SAO PAOLO

SAO PAOLO
(Brazil)

3   3   Brasileirão 27

Founding date: 1930/1935
Stadium: Estádio Cícero Pompeu de Toledo (Morumbi) (80,000 capacity)
Club colors: white, red, and black
Stars: Sani, Bellini, Cafu, Leonardo, Ceni, Kaká, Pato
Curiosity: São Paulo Futebol Clube is one of the most prestigious clubs in the world, the third in America, and the seventh in the world for international trophies won

BENFICA

LISBON
(Portugal)

2   33   Iª Liga 36

Founding date: 1904
Stadium: Estádio da Luz (66,000 capacity)
Club colors: white and red
Stars: Águas, Torres, Eusébio, Bento, João Pinto, Luiz, Preud'homme, Mozer, Nené, Rui Costa
Curiosity: the Portuguese team with the most trophies. At international level they have appeared in seven European Cup finals, winning two

PORTO

PORTO
(Portugal)

2   16   2   2   Iª Liga 27

Founding date: 1893
Stadium: Estádio do Dragão (52,000 capacity)
Club colors: blue and white
Stars: Cubillas, Madjer, Jardel, Vítor Baía, Deco, Carvalho, Costinha, Maniche, Ferreira, Postiga, Emanuel, Valente, Costa, Falcao, Hulk
Curiosity: the second Portuguese team in terms of the number of national titles won, but the first for international trophies

ARSENAL

LONDON
(England)

29   I   **Premier** 13

Founding date: 1886
Stadium: Emirates Stadium (60,000 capacity)
Club colors: white and red
Stars: Seaman, Dixon, Winterburn, Vieira, Campbell, Adams, Ljungberg, Brady, Henry, Bergkamp, Pirès
Curiosity: one of the richest and oldest clubs in the world, the most successful London team in terms of trophies. They hold the record for consecutive participation in the championship, from 1919 to today

LIVERPOOL

LIVERPOOL
(England)

5   30   3   **Premier** 18

Founding date: 1892
Stadium: Anfield (54,000 capacity)
Club colors: red
Stars: Kennedy, McDermott, Dalglish, Grobbelaar, Owen, Gerrard, Rush, Fowler, Barnes, Suárez
Curiosity: With 59 official trophies they are the second most successful English club after Manchester United, and one of the most successful in the world

MANCHESTER CITY

MANCHESTER
(England)

13   I   **Premier** 4

Founding date: 1880
Stadium: Etihad Stadium (55,000 capacity)
Club colors: white and light blue
Stars: Wright-Phillips, de Jong, Tévez, Adebayor, Kolo e Yaya Touré, Lescott, Agüero, Silva
Curiosity: hey won a lot in the 1960s and '70s, followed by a long decline; now, after a huge investment by their new Arab owners, they have returned to winning

ANDERLECHT

BRUSSELS
(Belgium)

10   I   2   **Pro League** 34

Founding date: 1908
Stadium: Constant Vanden Stock (22,000 capacity)
Club colors: white and purple
Stars: Van Himst, Haan, Rensenbrink, Vercauteren, Olsen, Munaron, Scifo, Kompany, Lukaku, De Sutter
Curiosity: the team with most trophies in Belgium, leading in terms of championships won, and one of the most famous at European level

Alberto Bertolazzi

started out as a journalist, first for radio and then in print, working on local and national titles, with glossy and travel magazines. As an author, he has taken part in the creation of educational and informative works devoted to the approach to sport and has produced numerous illustrated volumes of a historical, natural and artistic character. His debut as a novelist came in 2011, with *Il rugby salverà il mondo* (*Rugby will save the world*). He has practiced many sports, some at the competitive level (athletics, soccer, rugby), and others as an amateur (tennis, swimming, scuba diving). He has been a scuba instructor and president of an amateur soccer club, as well as a trainer and instructor for youth and children's teams in both soccer and rugby. He has collaborated with NuiNui Editions in the creation of various books for children, including Sports Explained to Children.

Originally published as *El Futbol explicado a los niños*, © 2018 by San Pablo

British Library Cataloguing in Publication Data
A catalogue record record for this book is available from the British Library

Soccer for Kids
Maidenhead: Meyer & Meyer Sport (UK) Ltd., 2018
ISBN 978-1-78255-150-8

© 2018 by Meyer & Meyer Sport (UK) Ltd.
Aachen, Auckland, Beirut, Cairo, Cape Town, Dubai, Hägendorf, Hong Kong, Indianapolis, Manila, Maidenhead, New Delhi, Singapore, Sydney, Teheran, Vienna

 Member of the World Sports Publishers' Association (WSPA), www.w-s-p-a.org

Credits:
Interior design: Danielle Stern
Layout: zerosoft
Cover artwork: Arianna Osti
Art director: Clara Zanotti

Translation: Contextus Srl, Pavia, Italy (Martin Maguire)
Managing Editor: Elizabeth Evans
Copyeditor: Anne Rumery
Printed by Print Consult GmbH, Munich, Germany

MIX
Paper from responsible sources
FSC® C084279

ISBN 978-1-78255-150-8
E-mail: info@m-m-sports.com
www.m-m-sports.com